gaz regan's
101 Best New Cocktails

Volume III

gaz regan's
101 Best New Cocktails

Volume III

gaz regan

mixellany limited

Copyright © 2013 Gary Regan

All rights reserved. Printed in the United Kingdom. No part of this book may be used or reproduced in any manner whatsoever without written permission except in the case of brief quotations embodied in critical articles and reviews. For information address Mixellany Limited, 3 Eyford Cottages, Upper Slaughter, Cheltenham, Gloucestershire GL54 2JL United Kingdom..

Mixellany books may be purchased for educational, business, or sales promotional use. For information, please write to Mixellany Limited, 3 Eyford Cottages, Upper Slaughter, Cheltenham, Gloucestershire GL54 2JL United Kingdom. or email jaredbrown1@mac.com

First edition

ISBN 13: 978-1-907434-42-6

British Library Cataloguing in Publication Data.
A catalogue record for this book is available from the British Library.

This book is dedicated to all the bartenders of the twenty-first century who have done so much to push the cocktailian envelope and bring us so many absolutely startling new drinks.

Acknowledgements

Thanks to all the bartenders who submitted recipes in 2013. Sorry if yours didn't make the cut, but please know that I had to choose 101 drinks out of over 7,000 sent to me over the past 12 months. Thanks, too, of course, to Martha, Anistatia, and Jared, and to all of you fabulous folk in the booze and/or bar business who make my life so much fun!

Table of Contents

Absolut Kelly by Ektoras Binikos	13
Aperitif by Joy Napolitano	16
Back Of The Cupboard Cocktail by Michael Stringer	18
Banana Buckmeister by Gorge Camorra	21
Bases Clearing Double by Sandy Levine	23
Battery Park Punch by Donnie Pratt	25
The Belfast Cocktail by Francis P. Schott	27
Bikers Grove by Jen Riley	30
Bird's Eye View by Steve Shur	34
Bitter Stripper by Dee Allen	36
Bittersweet Symphony Cocktail by Mariano Garcia Ibañez	38
Bloody Nail by Zachary Nelson	41
Bloomsbury Fizz by Giuseppe Santamaria	43
Bristol Old Fashioned N°2 by Maxime Hoerth	45
Bruschetta Martini by Eric Tecosky	48
The Charter Oak Cocktail by David A. Roth	50
Chaterhouse Cup	52
Chorizo and Cranberry Old-Fashioned by Joshua Powell	54
Coffee & Cigarettes by Jayce Kadyschuk	56
CuCuJulio by Francesco Cione	58
Cuidad Vieja by Alex Negranza	61

Cuzco Humming Bird by Moses Laboy	63
Delegation Cocktail by Carl Wenger	65
Dirty Margarita by Rob McHardy	66
Dolce & Verde by Charalabos "Babis" Spiridakis	69
Dutch Coupe by Tess Posthumus	71
El Habano by Julien Lopez	73
Ellipsis by Devender Sehgal	75
The Emperor by Valdez Campos	77
Fall Classic by Bob Brunner	78
53 Souvenirs by ms. franky marshallv	80
Free Rider by Billy Helmkamp	83
The Fruited Pig by Chad Larson	84
The Gentlemens' Secret by Giuseppe Santamaria	86
The Glorious Socialite by Benjamin Davies	88
Golden Prestige by Nicolas Michel	90
Good Night Sazerac	93
Grace Note by Seth Bregman	95
Green Hornet by Jesper Strauss	97
Gypsy Poem by Eric Grenier	99
Idle Hands by Payman Bahmani	101
Inked Zacapa Old Fashioned by Monica Berg	103
Irish Mermaid by Massimo La Rocca	105
Jack Jazz Rabbit by Marek Vojčarčik	107
Jake Barnes by Natalie Jacob	109
Jake Leg by Dimitris Kiakos	112
Jenkins! by Kate McDonald	114
La Croix Elixir by Humberto Marques	116
The Last Wynd by Sian Ferguson	118
Leaving Manhattan by Joanne Spiegel	120

Liberty Flip by Leo Lahti	123
McMillian by Geoffrey Wilson	125
The Merriweather Old-Fashioned by René Kronsteiner	126
Milord Gower by Frederic Yarm	128
Minty Silk by Diana Haider	130
Mont Blanc Cocktail by Lee Morris	132
Myrrah's Passion by Lindsay Laubenstein	134
Negrita by Giuseppe Gallo	137
The New Fashioned Old Fashioned by Jens Kerger	139
Norwegian Negroni	142
Norwegian Sour by Katrin Reitz	144
Not Coming Home by Tim Rabior	148
Old Fashioned No. 6 by Oron Lerner	150
Old Fashioned (Red House Style)	153
Old Quartermaster by Michael Shea	155
Papa Needs a New Pair of Shoes by Patrick Halloran	157
Paradise Punch by Cynthia Turner	160
Patriarch by Daniel Brancusi	162
Perfect Tickler by Carol Donovan	164
Pointy Reckoning by Claire Prideaux	167
Port of Spain by Kyle Mathis	169
Queen Anne's Revenge by Anthony DeSerio	171
Ready Room by Christopher Day	174
Red Barchetta by Mel James	176
Red Riding Hooch by Joseph Boley	178
Red Thorn Cocktail by Takumi Watanabe	179
Roark's Laughter by Chris Harrington	181
Rose Colored Glasses by Daniel Dufek	184
The Rusty Apple by Christopher James	186

Sazeroni by René Förster	188
Sencha Flip by Jason Walsh	190
Siam Saoco by Iain McPherson	192
Smokey Ol' Scribe by Tim Robinson	194
Smokin' Hopps by Seth Laufman	197
South of Heaven by George Megalokonomos	199
Spanish Inquisition by Scott Diaz	202
St. Joseph's by Chris Hannah	204
Strega Sour by Junior Ryan	206
A Tale of Two Roberts by Frank Caiafa	208
10 Bloods by Kelvin Wood	210
Third Day in Taipei by Aaron Feder	212
The Trainspotter by Thomas Newcomb	214
Trinity Avenue by Mark Holmes	216
Trott On by Nick Koumbarakis	218
A 23-year-old Girl by Foxyie Wong	220
A Two-Fold Operation by Phoebe Esmon	223
Vakantie by Cynthia Turner	225
War Of The Roses by Nick Caputo	227
Ward 9 by Jinjur Van Vogelpoel	231
The Westie by Fredo Ceraso	234
Where There's Smoke There's Fire by Leslie Ross	236
Wildbret by Reinhard Pohorec	240
Windsor Knot by Richard Yarnall	242
Yes Man by Scott Kennedy	244

Introduction

This project seems to have taken on a life of its own, and I'm learning so much about the cocktailian craft by reading all of the recipes that get sent to me, and testing all the drinks that tickle my fancy. It's a tough job, as they say, but . . .

Keep up the good work, bartenders!

Absolut Kelly

Adapted from a recipe by Ektoras Binikos, 2nd Floor on Clinton, New York

"I created the Absolut Kelly cocktail to be a transformative experience based on Joseph Beuys' idea of the 'anti-image'. The outward appearance of the Absolut Kelly—with its gray, muted tones—belies its combination of unexpectedly colorful, complex flavors. All components were carefully selected to represent the ethos and sensibilities of this great art institution that is the Sean Kelly Gallery." —Ektoras Binikos

45 ml (1.5 oz) Absolut vodka
15 ml (5 oz) Becherovka
30 ml (1 oz) lime juice
30 ml (1 oz) yuzu juice
45 ml (1.5 oz) gum Arabic syrup or simple syrup
3 shiso leaves (2 for garnish)
2 lime wedges
4 drops of Mastiha water
3 drops of Hella Citrus Bitters
3 drops of Bergamot Bitters
Meyer lemon zest (or lemon/lime zest)
100 mg of activated charcoal powder
Smoked sea salt for garnish
In a martini shaker, muddle 2 lime wedges, one shiso leaf, the gum Arabic syrup and the Mastiha water. Add ice and remaining ingredients except for the Bergamot bitters. Shake well. Strain

into a high ball glass filled with ice and rimmed with smoked sea salt. Garnish with 2 shiso leaves and top with 2-3 drops of Bergamot bitters.

gaz sez: *I've been wondering how long it would take before someone created a drink that would be a transformative experience based on Joseph Beuys' idea of the 'anti-image,' and of course, there's only one bartender in the known universe who would tackle this job. Ektoras Binikos is the most creative bartender I ever did come across, and I'm so impressed that an artist of his caliber chose to use cocktails as a vehicle for some of his work. Get yourself down to the 2nd Floor on Clinton in NYC and be prepared to be impressed. Be prepared to be very impressed.*

gaz also sez: *It's hard for me to express just how honored I believe the bartending world is to have an artist of the caliber of Ektoras choose to use cocktails as one of his mediums. He's one very special guy.*

And in response to a couple of questions, Ektoras added: "The charcoal goes into the shaker like the rest of the ingredients and you just shake and strain into a high ball filled with new ice. No need for a cheesecloth. The active charcoal adds no flavor to the cocktail is purely visual.

"The cocktail is very conceptually based. All components were selected to represent the ethos and sensibilities of the Sean Kelly Gallery which is very much a conceptual based gallery. The visual aspect of the cocktail was very important to me. I wanted to create visually something very provocative . . . [and] I took inspiration from Joseph Beuys, a great German conceptual artist

that I admire. J B used lots of gray in his work . . . He had a theory based on the idea of the 'anti-image' and by using gray he tried to make you see colors. 'So it isn't right to say I'm interested in gray. That's not right. And I'm not interested in dirt either. I'm interested in a process which reaches much further,' Beuys said.

"So the goal here was to create a transformative experience. The outward appearance of the drink with its gray muted tones - belies its combination of unexpected complex flavors creating a lucid and colorful experience.

"The medicinal properties of the active charcoal as a natural detoxifier render it a survival elixir in the Beuys tradition.

"Also as a mixologist and visual artist I have this idea that my cocktails are components of a large social sculpture. I love the way people interact around them and [this] is a very meaningful process to me. At the Sean Kelly inaugural gala you had the impression that people were holding little statues referential to a black winged Victory of Samothrace.

PS: Drinking the Absolut Kelly may cause temporary darkening of the stool."

Aperitif

Adapted from a recipe by Joy Napolitano, Elle Restaurant, Rome, Italy.

"This drink was created for the Campari bartender competition in Italy. The mix of ingredients is really delicious. The Campari is the main element and the other ingredients exalts its flavor. The co2 will give us the freshness of this drink and the bubbles emanate a real fragrance of elderflower and citrus,"—Joy Napolitano

40 ml (1.3 oz) Campari
30 ml (1 oz) Noilly Prat original Dry vermouth
30 ml (1 oz) St. Germaine elderflower liqueur
orange and lemon twists, as garnishes

Using appropriate equipment, put these ingredients together, including the twists, and carbonate the drink. Or shake over ice and strain into a chilled cocktail glass. Add the garnishes.

gaz sez: *I made a batch of these in my soda-stream machine and they went down real well at a friend's party. Nice and simple. And delicious.*

Back Of The Cupboard Cocktail

Adapted from a recipe by Michael Stringer, Michael-Stringer.com & Hire The Barman, London

"I wanted to create a twist on one of my favourite cocktails, the sours. The herbal flavours of the Chartreuse blend perfectly with the smooth kick of the Naked Grouse whisky, while the lemon and bitters provide a citrus undertone to the drink. The egg white finishes off with a smooth, creamy texture. This cocktail was featured in both Simon Difford's **Class Magazine** and also **Bar Magazine** in the UK." —Michael Stringer.

40 ml (1.35 oz) Yellow Chartreuse VEP
15 ml (.5 oz) Naked Grouse scotch whisky
20 ml (.7 oz) egg white
20 ml (.7 oz) fresh lemon juice
10 ml (.35 oz) gomme syrup
2 dashes Regans' Orange Bitters No. 6
1 grapefruit twist, as garnish

Add all of the ingredients to a cocktails shaker with the spring of a hawthorne strainer and dry shake hard. Take the spring out, fill with ice, and shake hard again. Double strain into an ice-filled rocks glass. add the garnish. filled with ice.

gaz sez: *I confess I'd never heard of Naked Grouse scotch, and it's a darned tasty dram. Here's what the distillery has to say about it: "As the makers of The Famous Grouse we bring over 100 years of whisky making to the creation of The Naked Grouse. We have enriched the best loved flavours of Scotland's Favourite Whisky by maturing our blend in hard to find (and pricey!) sun dried sherry oak casks. Distinctively sweet, rich and, some* would say, famously smooth – The Naked Grouse is simply pure indulgence in a bottle."

As for the cocktail, it's simply divine. I love the way the Chartreuse dances with the scotch here (and this recipe also works well without the lemon juice, egg white, and gomme if you, like me, aren't a massive fan of citrus).

Banana Buckmeister

Adapted from a recipe by Gorge Camorra, Cloud9 bar, Geelong, Victoria, Australia

45 ml (1.5 oz) Jägermeister
15 ml (.5 oz) Joseph Catron banana liqueur
60 ml (2 oz) freshly pressed orange juice
3 dashes Regans orange bitters
1 orange twist, as garnish
Shake over ice and strain into a chilled cocktail glass. Add the garnish

gaz sez: *I met Gorge at the 2013 G'Vine Gin Connoisseurs bartender competition, and he impressed all hell out of me. He's not only a fabulous bartender and a creative genius, he's an all-around good guy who takes lots of time to help others in his community. This drink is just spectacular, and the idea of marrying Jägermeister and banana liqueur is just inspired. I confess to not using the specific brand of liqueur that Gorge specifies when I tested this one, but I dare say that the drink will work well with near-as-darn-it any brand. Nicely done, Gorge. I'm proud to call you my friend on so many levels.*

Bases Clearing Double

THE RECIPES

Adapted from a recipe by Sandy Levine, The Oakland, Ferndale, MI

60 ml (2 oz) Gingerbread Rooibus-
Infused Bulleit Rye*
22 ml (.75 oz) orgeat
22 ml (.75 oz) fresh orange juice
22 ml (.75 oz) fresh lime juice
22 ml (.75 oz) pineapple juice
freshly grated nutmeg, as garnish
Shake over ice and strain into a crushed-ice-filled collins glass. Add the garnish.

*Gingerbread Rooibus-Infused Bulleit Rye
Infuse 1 bottle Bulleit Rye with 1 tablespoon of Rare Tea Cellar's Gingerbread Dream Rooibus Tea for 3 hours. Strain and reserve.

gaz sez: *The infused rye is a stroke of genious. It works very well indeed in this drink, and I'm betting it will work well in Manhattan and Old-Fashioned variations, too. Nice touch, Sandy.*

Battery Park Punch

Adapted from a recipe by Donnie Pratt, Cucina 24, Asheville, North Carolina

45 ml (1.5 oz) Leblon Cachaça
22 ml (.75 oz) fresh pineapple juice
15 ml (.5 oz) fresh lemon juice
15 ml (.5 oz) gunpowder green tea infused honey
15 ml (.5 oz) Fernet Branca
Club Soda
fresh grated nutmeg, as garnish

Shake all the ingredients except for the soda water over ice and strain into an ice-filled double old-fashioned glass. Top with club soda, stir briefly, and add the garnish.

gaz sez: *This one really knocked my socks off--green tea, honey, and Fernet Branca are true soul-mates. It's a combination that should be remembered. The cachaça works well here, too, and I imagine that the drink would also fare well with pisco, or even tequila. Might be worth a spin, huh?*

Gunpowder Green Tea Infused Honey

Steep two tablespoons loose-leaf Gunpowder Green Tea in 10 oz. of not quite boiling water for five minutes. Strain into 10 oz. of honey, stir until incorporated, bottle, and refrigerate.

Belfast Cocktail

Adapted from a recipe by Francis P. Schott, co-owner of Catherine Lombardi and Stage Left restaurants in New Brunswick.

"I've got a cocktail for your consideration. It's called The Belfast Cocktail. It's inspired by the Brandy and Port that always seems to end the night when I am in that fair city. I was recently appointed an official ambassador of the City of Belfast and I'm putting together a sister-city relationship with New Brunswick. Last month, I had Lord Mayor Máirtín Ó Muilleoir to my restaurant, to meet with New Brunswick's own Mayor Jim Cahill and about 20 or so of our local business and government leaders over a fine lunch in our wine library. At the invitation of Lord Mayor Ó Muilleoir, in January Mayor Cahill will lead a delegation of a dozen or so business leaders to Belfast. We will attempt to set up some lasting exchanges in our arts, theater, music, financial development, university, government sectors, restaurants and bars (my bailiwick). At the luncheon in New Brunswick, we served The Belfast Cocktail. Lord Mayor Ó Muilleoir and all the guests loved it. In Belfast we will have the same. It is my hope to see this drink popularized on both cities. Plus it's delicious. It is on our cocktail menu." —Francis P. Schott

45 ml (1.5 oz) Ruby Port
45 ml (1.5 oz) Cognac (Hennessy VS)
15 ml (.5 oz) Poire Williams (Purkhart)
15 ml (.5 oz) Cinnamon Syrup*
1 dash Bitter Truth Orange Bitters
1 orange twist, as garnish
1 dash Dale DeGroff's Pimento bitters,
as an aromatic garnish

Stir over ice, and strain into a chilled cocktail glass. Flame the orange twist and add it to the glass, and add a dash of Dale DeGroff's Pimento bitters, as an aromatic garnish.

*Cinnamon Syrup
1 cup sugar
1 cup Water
1 cinnamon stick
Put ingredients into a pan and heat and stir till sugar is dissolved. Continue to keep over low heat for 5-10 minutes until it becomes cinnamon-y

gaz sez: *Port and Brandy has been a favorite of mine for decades, and this new look at the drink is pretty spectacular. The Poire Williams give it a fabulous kiss on the lips and bring the whole thing to life. Nicely done, Francis.*

Bikers Grove

Adapted from a recipe by Jen Riley, Red House/Le Tiki Lounge, Paris

"I was working for Candelaria at the point of conception of the Biker's Grove and was invited to work for a large annual spirits event called Whiskey Live organised by Le Maison du Whisky in the September of last year (2012). I was to be representing Tequila Ocho and asked to create a cocktail using the 2011 blanco. I love the ideology of Ocho (producing tequila in the same manner that wine is produced and seeing just how much the 'terroir' affects the agave and the final outcome of the tequila) I wanted to create a fairly dry drink that would accentuate the earthiness of the tequila. I played about with variations on other classics such as the Negroni and Manhattan but nothing seemed to do the tequila justice for me. Then one night, rooting around the back of the fridge, I pulled out a bottle of aquavit and thought why not give it a go? I immediately the loved the play-off between the caraway notes of the aquavit and the earthy spice of the Ocho, and so maraschino and grapefruit were added and the Bikers Grove was born. I decided to express the oils from the grapefruit zest onto the interior of the glass, as when expressed onto the surface of the drink, the scent of the grapefruit overwhelmed the herbal and vegetal notes i was trying to highlight. Expressing the oils onto the interior of the glass added a fresh awakening note to the cocktail without being over powering. I was also lucky enough to spend an evening with Tomas Estes at Candelaria. Myself and my boyfriend (Joe) were out getting tacos there, when Adam (one of Candelarias owners) passed through and told me Tomas was in the bar enjoying my cocktail and that I should come on through to say hello. We bobbed our heads in to say hello and ended up drinking a great deal of Bikers Groves. Anecdotes were shared and the wonderful soiree saw Tomas and Joe arm wrestling in a candle lit corner of the bar! Brilliant

1 grapefruit twist
50 ml (1.7 oz) Ocho tequila blanco 2011
20 ml (.66 oz) aquavit
1 barspoon Luxardo maraschino liqueur
2 dashes Scrappy's grapefruit bitters
1 green olive, as garnish
Serve in a chilled martini glass
Express the oil of the grapefruit twist onto the interior of a chilled cocktail glass, and discard the zest. Stir the remaining ingredients over ice, strain into the pre-prepared glass, and add the garnish.

gaz sez: *Love the story behind this drink, and I'm so jealous that I wasn't with Jen, Tomas, and Joe at Candelaria that night. At least I've been able to sample this drink, though, and it's a* *veritable doozy of a cocktail. Ocho is such a fabulous tequila, and Jen merely decorates it with tiny tapestries of flavors that make this drink taste like a fine old country-western song. There's a banjo here, fiddles over there, a harmonica pipes up now and then, and you can hear washboards in the background keeping the beat. Nice one, Jen.*

Bird's Eye View

Adapted from a recipe by Steve Shur, Boston College Club, Boston, Ma

"Very nice balance here. 4 great spirits that taste great together. [This drink is] loved by many." —Steve Shur.

45 ml (1.5 oz) Eagle Rare Bourbon
22.5 ml (.75 oz) Ramazzotti Amaro
15 ml (.5 oz) Carpano Antica Formula

7.5 ml (.25 oz) Yellow Chartreuse
1 lemon twist, as an aromatic garnish.
Stir over ice and strain into a chilled wine glass. Twist the lemon twist over surface and discard.

gaz sez: *Incredibly nice balance, Steve. The amaro and the Chartreuse take the vanilla edge off the Carpano very well, indeed. Plus, it's hard to go wrong with Eagle Rare, right?*

Bitter Stripper

Adapted from a recipe by Dee Allen , 399, Perth, Australia

"This drink is based on the negroni. The intention was to replicate the flavours of a negroni without using campari or a sweet vermouth, to create a clear drink." —Dee Allen

40ml (1.3 oz) Plymouth Gin
15ml (.5 oz) Dolin Blanc
10ml (.3 oz) Salers Gentiane
5ml (.15 oz) Cointreau
1 orange twist, as garnish
Stir all ingredients over ice, and strain into a chilled martini glass. Zest the orange peel over the glass, twist and balance on the rim as the garnish.

gaz sez: *Weird and wonderful, is this drink. Weird and wonderful.*

Bittersweet Symphony Cocktail

Adapted from a recipe by Mariano Garcia Ibañez, Banker's Bar, Mandarin Oriental, Barcelona.

"As the cocktail was made for "Angostura cocktail challenge 2013" i wanted to find a way for using the bitters in a considerable quantity, so the mixture with the sweetness of the Cherry Heering and the spices syrup was the key. Some sour added with the lemon juice and the main personality by the hand of the Caribbean rum. Why is it called "bittersweet symphony?" i could say because that name fits with the flavours, but it's basically because i love that song ;)" —Mariano Garcia Ibañez.

45 ml (1.5 oz) Angostura 1919 Rum
30 ml (1 oz) Cherry Heering

30 ml (1 oz) lemon juice
25 ml (.85 oz) cinnamon syrup
15 ml (.5 oz) white and red pepper syrup
24 dashes (.5 oz) Angostura bitters
1 cinnamon stick, as garnish
1 Manhattan-infused cherry, as garnish
freshly grated nutmeg, as garnish
Shake over ice and strain into an ice-filled highball glass. Add the garnishes.

Cinnamon Syrup
1 liter (34 oz) water
1 kg (2.2 lbs) sugar
8 to 10 cinnamon sticks (depending on size and quality)
Combine the ingredients in a non-reactive saucepan and heat, stirring frequently, until the sugar is dissolved. Simmer for 10 minutes, remove from the heat, allow to cool, and store in the refrigerator.

White And Red Pepper Syrup
1 liter (34 oz) water
1 kg (2.2 lbs) sugar
70 grams (2.5 oz) red peppercorns
30 grams (1 oz) white peppercorns
Combine the ingredients in a non-reactive saucepan and heat, stirring frequently, until the sugar is dissolved. Simmer for 10 minutes, remove from the heat, allow to cool, and store in the refrigerator.

gaz sez: *How can you go wrong when you throw half-an-ounce of Angostura in there? Seriously, though, it's Mariano's White and*

Red Pepper Syrup that pulls everything together in this baby. It's an inspired touch. Try it. You'll like it.

Bloody Nail

Adapted from a recipe by Zachary Nelson, The Continental Room, Fullerton, CA

"Part Rusty Nail and part Blood and Sand. I was making a Rusty Nail for a customer and as I was pouring the Drambuie, I looked up at the Cherry Heering and thought I'd give it a shot," Zachary Nelson.

60 ml (2 oz) Dewar's White Label scotch
15 ml (.5 oz) Drambuie
15 ml (.5 oz) Cherry Heering
2 dashes Regans' Orange Bitters No. 6
1 flamed orange peel, as garnish
Stir over ice and strain into an ice-filled old-fashioned glass. Add the garnish.

gaz sez: *Another of those simple drinks that works so damned well, this Bloody Nail will have bartenders all over the world slapping their foreheads saying, "Why didn't I think of that."*

Bloomsbury Fizz

Adapted from a recipe by Giuseppe Santamaria, Boutique Bar / Ohla Hotel, Barcelona, Spain.

"This cocktail is a modern version of a Fizz. Its name is inspired by the London district where Charles Tanqueray founded a small distillery in 1830 and Tanqueray was born.

This drink uncovers the sharpness of the citrus flavour of this gin, combined with the summery, fresh notes of basil, perfectly balanced with the velvet warm of the port. Perfect at any time the day. (Cocktail winner the Spanish Tanqueray Ten World Class Semifinal 2010.)" —Giuseppe Santamaria.

6 fresh basil leaves (reserve 1 for garnish)
20 ml (.66 oz) gomme syrup
40 ml (1.33 oz) Tanqueray No. TEN gin
10 ml (.33 oz) fresh lemon juice
10 ml (.33 oz) fresh lime juice
1 large egg white
Dash soda water
20 ml (.66 oz) ruby port
a few basil leaves, as garnish

Smash the basil with the syrup in a mixing glass. Add ice, the gin, egg white, and lemon and lime juices. Shake vigorously and double-strain into a chilled coupette. Float the port then add the soda to the mixing glass to create a

foam (in contact with the remains of the egg white) and float this foam on top.
Add the garnish.

gaz sez: *Tricky little number is this one--I'm not the best layerer in the business. Once it's assembled, though, this is a stunningly fabulous drink—the T10 and the basil run a triathlon on the palate as they swim around and do a few wheelies before sprinting down the throat. Masterpiece material is this baby.*

Bristol Old Fashioned N°2

Adapted from a recipe by Maxime Hoerth, Le Bar du Bristol, Paris, France

"This cocktail reminds me of my childhood. Born in Alsace (north-east of France) I grew up with the X-mas flavours and I wanted to join those flavours to my favorite cocktail that is the old-fashioned (made with rum, gin, cognac, bourbon ...). This is how and why that cocktail was created. X-mas flavours in a gentleman cold drink." —Maxime Hoerth.

15 ml (1/2 oz) Hot Wine shrub*
3 dashes Burlesque Bitters
50 ml (1.7 oz) Gosling's Black Seal rum
1 cinnamon stick, as garnish
1 star anise, as garnish
1 orange twist, as garnish
Pour the shrub and the bitters into a chilled old-fashioned glass. Add half of the rum and a few ice cubes and stir. Add more ice and the second half of the rum. Add the garnishes.

*Hot Wine Shrub

70 ml (2.4 oz) St-Emilion Bordeaux Wine
150 ml (5 oz) Grand Marnier Cordon Rouge
150ml (5 oz) Wild Strawberry Liqueur
3 cinnamon sticks
4 orange slices
4 cloves

3 star anise

Heat all ingredients and let reduce until half of it has evaporated. Filter, add 185 ml (.8 cup) caster (superfine) sugar, and stir to dissolve. Allow to cool and refrigerate.

gaz sez: *Jeez this was a bitch to put together, but it was well worth all the effort. Maxime, who I know from my travels, has, indeed, put Christmas in a glass here, and here's no need to wait for cold weather to drink it, either.*

P.S.: Try the shrub in your coffee of a morning. It's pretty deeeelish!

Bruschetta Martini

Adapted from a recipe by Eric Tecosky, Jones Hollywood, West Hollywood, CA.

"Everyone's favorite appetizer is now their favorite cocktail. Form meets function in this perfect start to any dinner party. Enjoy!!!" —Eric Tecosky

2 cherry tomatoes
60 ml (2 oz) Beluga vodka
7.5 ml (.25 oz) Dirty Sue premium olive juice
15 ml (.5 oz) fresh lemon juice
1 basil leaf
1 small slice of garlic
pinch of salt
pinch of black pepper

Muddle the tomatoes in a mixing glass, the add the remaining ingredients, reserving one of the basil leaves for a garnish. Add ice and shake well for 10 to 15 seconds. Strain into a chilled cocktail glass through a fine-mesh strainer, and add the basil-leaf garnish.

gaz sez: *I used a different vodka and different olive juice, but this one worked real well despite my sloppiness. I love savory drinks that aren't Bloody Marys. Nice one, Eric!*

The Charter Oak Cocktail

Adapted from a recipe by David A. Roth, Pigs Eye Pub, Hartford, Connecticut

"This drink is inspired by Colonial Connecticut and named after the Charter Oak Tree that stood in Hartford until 1856. The Colonists hid the state charter (the precursor to the county's Constitution) in the oak tree from Kings James II in 1687.

"The Rum is for the 5 Rum distilleries that CT had by the 1750's.

"The Akvavit is for the Dutch that settled Hartford in the early 1600's.

"The Chartreuse is for the French General Lafayette who was our ally in the Revolutionary War.

"The lemon juice is for brightness and the nutmeg is for aromatics and spice and also because Connecticut is also nicknamed the Nutmeg State. Cheers!" —David A. Roth

> 30 ml (1 oz.) Don Q. Cristal Rum
> 30 ml (1 oz.) Aalborg Akvavit
> 30 ml (1 oz.) Yellow Chartreuse
> 15 ml (.5 oz.) Fresh Lemon Juice
> freshly grated nutmeg, as garnish
> Shake over ice and strain into a chilled
> coupe glass. Add the garnish.

gaz sez: *Akvavit and Chartreuse in the same glass? Who'd have thunk it? They're like a well-choreographed ice-skating couple, anticipating each other's every move, and complimenting each nuance. Very nicely done, David.*

Charterhouse Cup

Adapted from a recipe by Adrian Gomes, The Corpse and Cocktail, Aberdeen, Scotland.

"This creation was a regional finalist for a UK competition held in Edinburgh by cult French liqueur, Chartreuse. Although the drink didn't reach the UK final, it received an honourable mention by 'UK Bartender of the Year (2011)' Jamie MacDonald of The Raconteur, Stockbridge, citing the drink as his favourite on the day." —Adrian Gomes.

25 ml (.83 oz) green Chartreuse
15 ml (.5 oz) Pimm's No. 1 Cup
10 ml (.33 oz) Trois Rivieres rhum (or any unaged or young rhum agricole)
20 ml (.66 oz) fresh lemon juice
2 teaspoons granulated sugar

1 dash egg white
1 cucumber ribbon, folded repeatedly
and threaded onto a cocktail stick and
topped with a mint leaf, as garnish

Dry-shake, then add ice and shake again. Fine-strain into a chilled small wine goblet. Add the garnish.

gaz sez: *This is an interesting quaff. It's weird to witness the Chartreuse teasing the Pimm's Cup on the palate until, just a couple of seconds later, the rhum jumps into the fray and the waters are stilled. Nicely played, Adrian.*

Chorizo and Cranberry Old-Fashioned

Adapted from a recipe by Joshua Powell, Bar 44, Penarth, South Glamorgan, Welsh Wales, UK.

"This cocktail is finely balanced with aromatic spicy, nutty, woody, and sweet flavours. It was made as part of a Christmas menu for Bar 44 and being a Spanish style Tapas bar, it went down a treat." —Joshua Powell

45 ml (1.5 oz) Chorizo-infused Bulleit Bourbon*
15 ml (.5 oz) Cranberry Vodka
1 dash Angostura Bitters
2 Dashes Angostura Orange Bitters
7.5 ml (.25 oz) Gomme syrup
40 ml (1 oz) Cranberry juice
1 Chorizo and Orange peel skewer, as garnish

Stir over ice and strain into an ice-filled Old-Fashioned glass. Add the garnish.

***Chorizo infused Bourbon:**, fry off some diced spanish chorizo in a small amount of oil for a few minutes. Add a tablespoon of Picante (hot) paprika. Stir well and then collect the oil. Add 6 ounces of chorizo oil for every 70cl bottle of bourbon. I used Bulleit as I find other sweeter varieties added too much nutty taste to the end product. Let sit and stir occasionally then put in the freezer for 2 hours to set the fat. When fat has separated, remove it from bourbon and filter it through coffee paper.

gaz sez: *This one was just too crazy to ignore, right? Chorizo-infused Bulleit bourbon, indeed! Mind you, I do love chorizo, and I loves me some Bulleit bourbon, too, so . . . This drink will knock your socks off. I never tasted anything like it in my life. Just fabulous.*

Coffee & Cigarettes

Adapted from a recipe by Jayce Kadyschuk, Clive's Classic Lounge, Victoria, Canada

"I created this cocktail to represent Columbia on our new "Global Cocktails" concept menu at Clive's Classic Lounge. Creating cocktails that represent; traditional culinary & beverage flavors, and with the Coffee & Cigarettes Cocktail - goods produced & exported. As Columbia is known for its exports of both coffee and tobacco products. To be cheeky, and with the right guests, I'll add the small powdered sugar rim to represent another, not so legal, export Columbia is known for. It always draws a laugh and allows me to interact about our approach to the global concept menu and the fun we had coming up with the cocktails."— Jayce Kadyschuk

45 ml (1.5 oz) McClellends Islay Scotch (Bowmore 12)
15 ml (.5 oz) Luxardo Amaro Abano
15 ml (.5 oz) Cold brew Columbian coffee
1 dash Scrappy's Chocolate Bitters
1 bar spoon simple syrup
1 brandied cherry, as garnish

Rim 1/6 of the edge of a chilled coupe with powdered sugar; stir all the ingredients over ice, and strain into the prepared glass. Add the garnish.

gaz sez: *I had no McClelland's scotch so I used a Bowmore 12-year-old (McClellands is made at the Bowmore distillery). I used my regular coffee which is Dean's Beans Italian Espresso Roast. This baby worked perfectly so I've now found another scotch-based drink that I'm sure I'll go back to over and over again. Nicely done, Jayce!*

CuCuJulio

Adapted from a recipe by Francesco Cione, Caffè Baglioni at the Carlton Hotel, Milano, Italy.

"[This was the] winning Cocktail recipe at the recent DIAGEO World Class Italian semi-final held in Milan last April, 2, 2013. Inspired by the Mexican cucumber flavored "Agua Fresca de Pepino" drink and, of course, by a new classic Tommy's Margarita. The cocktail, as you can see from the picture, has been served in a special box with an open glass cover. This would represent a cocktail shown in a 'shop window.' The drink is served with an Hibiscus flower in syrup on the side that can be added to the drink to give a rounder and sweeter. An orchid flower and some fresh lemongrass supported into the box complete the cocktail presentation."— Francesco Cione.

50 ml (1.7 oz) Don Julio Reposado
10 ml (.3 oz) freshly squeezed lime juice
10 ml (.3 oz) homemade vanilla flavored sugar syrup
3 large fresh cucumber chunks
5 drops Pimiento Dram
1 pink grapefruit twist, as garnish

Muddle the cucumber well in a tin, add ice, and the remaining ingredients, and roll between the tin and a mixing glass until well mixed and well chilled. Strain into a chilled Orléans- style stem glass, or other stylish wine glass, and add the garnish.

"Serve with a smile and an extra dash of love free included." —Francesco Cione.

gaz sez: *Good Golly Miss Molly! This is such a fine drink, and I think it might be the way that the Pimiento Dram plays with the Don Julio and the cucumber, that really makes it stand out. Nicely done, Francesco!*

Cuidad Vieja

Adapted from a recipe by Alex Negranza, Liberty Bar, Seattle

"This drink was inspired by the Vieux Carre. I had a customer who loved them and Sazeracs, but they wanted something more viscous but still spirit forward," —Alex Negranza.

30 ml (1 oz) Laird's Bottled in Bond
applejack
22.5 ml (3/4 oz) dry curacao
15 ml (1/2 oz) Ron Zacapa 23
7.5 ml (1/4 oz) Bénédictine
2 dashes Creole bitters*
1 lemon twist, as garnish

Build in double old-fashioned glass. Stir until well chilled, and add the garnish.

*Substitute Peychaud's if Creole bitters aren't available.

gaz sez: *My style of drink, this is. I'll take one as an after-work drink, and another as a nightcap, thank you. I could drink these all night, if truth be told.*

Cuzco Humming Bird

Adapted from a recipe by Moses Laboy, Los Americanos, New York.

"This a fantastic, refreshing cocktail with a nice energy kick :) I hope to see my cocktail/name among the other great 100 cocktails," —Moses Laboy.

60 ml (2oz) Pisco brandy
22.5 ml (.75 oz) coca-tea simple syrup*
7.5 ml (.25 oz) mint simple syrup
22.5 ml (.75 oz) fresh lemon juice
2 dashes Angostura bitters
1 fresh mint sprig, as garnish

Pour into a large tiki/piragua glass. Add crushed ice, swizzle, top with more ice, garnish and serve.

*Coca-Tea Simple Syrup

Infuse 10 Coca tea bags and 2 yerba mate tea bags in .6 litre (2 1/2 cups) boiling water, and add .3 liter (1 1/3 cups) granulated sugar, and stir to dissolve. Allow to cool to room temperature and store in the refrigerator.

gaz sez: *I had no idea that coca tea was legal here in the USA, and boy, oh boy, does it work well in this drink. Brings back fabulous memories of the Urubamba Valley when I visited Peru with Diego and Elisa Loret de Mola a few years ago. I'll be sipping this one on a regular basis.*

Delegation Cocktail

Adapted from a recipe by Carl Wenger, Shady Lady Saloon, Sacramento, CA

45 ml (1.5oz) Camus VS Cognac
22.5 ml (.75oz) Choya Ume Excellent liqueur*
22.5 ml (.75oz) Averna amaro
1 brandied cherry, as garnish
Stir over ice and strain into chilled coupe. Add the garnish.

* Choya Ume Excellent liqueur is made with a plum-like fruit called *ume*, and it's often described as a plum brandy. It's a delicious fruit liqueur that deserves more space behing the bars of today's cocktailian bartenders.

gaz sez: *Simple, elegant, and very, very more-ish. And this is one of those cocktails that can be tailored to suit everyone. Go up on the plum brandy if you have a sweet tooth, go up on the Averno if you lean toward bitter, or use less of either one of them to please your palate. This cocktail will have your guests coming back for more for a long, long time.*

Dirty Margarita

Adapted from a recipe by Rob McHardy, Silencio, Paris, France.

"I use Cocktail Kingdom barspoons, which are roughly 3.4 to 4 ml to measure.
The caper juice is strong enough to destroy the drink if even slightly more is added. But totally makes it when I get it right. Enjoy!" —Rob McHardy.

50 ml (1.65 oz) Tequila Ocho plata
20 ml (.66 oz) fresh lime juice
20 ml (.66 oz) Cointreau
4 ml (.13 oz) agave syrup (uncut)
3 ml (.1 oz) caper juice*
1 lime twist, as garnish

Shake well over ice and double-strain into a chilled cocktail glass. Add the garnish.

*Caper Juice: I just had a chat with my wonderful olive supplier here in Paris. They are Sicilians with a very intimate relationship with their suppliers back home and their shop la tete dans les olives in the 11th arrondissement is well worth a visit. They made the juice by taking quite a large quantity of capers and putting them in a bucket with holes in the bottom (to capture the juice), covering them with salt and letting osmosis draw the juice from the capers over time. Either that or get a load of capers in salt and press like mad/dance/sit /jump on them to extract the juice. They are not aware of anyone else doing this or at least bottling it (it does smell pretty rank).

gaz sez: *Rob is right about being careful with the caper juice in this one, and he also made a good decision when he decided to call for Tequila Ocho Plata—a fabulous bottling that comes on real strong in any sort of Margarita, Rosita, or Paloma. I had a great night in Paris with Rob when Monkey Shoulder scotch flew me out there to conduct a Mindful Bartender workshop. Rob is the real deal.*

Dolce & Verde

Adapted from a recipe by Charalabos "Babis" Spiridakis, Cocktail Bar Passo Doble, Mykonos, Greece.

"The bar that I work for seven years now it's in a hot island of Greece called Mykonos. That's why I wanted a refreshing cocktail that is served in a glass full of ice but so tasty that in a hot day, somebody can drink it before the ice melts.

"Thank you Gary for the incredible work you are doing. I have learned a lot from your books and from the excellent bartenders that expose their work through you. Keep it going." —Babis Spridakis.

50 ml (1.65 oz) Stolichnaya vodka
40 ml (1.33 oz) homemade green apple puree
35 ml (1.17 oz) fresh lemon juice
20 ml (.66 oz) maraschino liqueur
25 ml (.83 oz) Monin cucumber syrup
Soda water, to fill
1 cucumber slice, as garnish
1 mint sprig, as garnish
Shake over ice and strain into a highball glass filled with ice. Top with soda water and add the garnishes.

gaz sez: *This is so not my style of drink. And this is so fabulous I wish that I lived on Mykonos so I could drink it all summer long. Well done, Babis. This is a brilliant creation.*

Dutch Coupe

Adapted from a recipe by Tess Posthumus, Door 74, Amsterdam, The Netherlands

"When Queen Beatrix announced she'll abdicate the throne on 30 April 2013, I thought the occasion called for a special cocktail in her name. The drink is based on a typical Dutch spirit and uses orange to accentuate the royal house of Orange-Nassau.

"The addition of some bitterness is part of a tradition. The Dutch royals used to drink a bitter orange liqueur called 'Oranjebitter' whenever there was a festive event. After zesting the orange, place it as a garnish on the rim and make it look like a feathered hat, which is Queen Beatrix' signature."
—Tess Posthumus

60ml (2 oz) Bols 6-year-old Corenwyn Jenever
15ml (.5 oz) Carpano Antica Formula
10ml (.33 oz) Cynar
1 dash orange flower water
1 dash orange bitters
1 orange twist, as garnish

Stir over ice, and strain into a frozen coupe glass. Add the garnish.

gaz sez: *Depending on where in the world you are, the 6-year-old Corenwyn Jenever might prove difficult to find, and it's really the backbone of this drink, so if you'd like to taste the Dutch Coupe as Tess intended it, I advise you to hold off until you find some, or take a trip to Amsterdam and have Ms. Posthumus fix you one her own self. You won't regret it. Promise.*

El Habano

Adapted from a recipe by Julien Lopez, Papa Doble, Montpellier, France

"[I'm a] big fan of rum and cigars, [so] the idea of this cocktail was to reproduce the entire range of aromatic Cuban cigars through a beverage of character. To do this I use an old rum with rich aromas, Pedro Ximenez sherry for notes of dried fruit, and to add complexity, bitters aged in oak whiskey barrels for aromatic persistence and a little bit of brown sugar molasses. The glass is sprayed with particularly peaty whiskey to make any side "cigar burn" to the entire cocktail. Finally, a long orange peel will take place to provide the necessary freshness. This Cocktail is on the Papa Doble (Cocktail bar from Montpellier) menu for more than a year and was recognized in 2012 trophies bar in France," —Julien Lopez.

Ardbeg 10-year-old scotch, to rinse the glass
50 ml (1.7 oz) Banks "7 Golden Age" rum
50 ml (1.7 oz) brown sugar canne syrup
50 ml (1.7 oz) Pedro Ximenez sherry
4 dashes Fee Brothers Whiskey Barrel Aged Bitters
Sweet spices (Cinnamon, star anise, cocoa)
1 orange twist, as garnish

Rinse a whisky-tasting glass with the

Ardbeg, then stir the ingredients over ice, and strain into the prepared glass. Add the garnish.

gaz sez: *This is my kinda drink. Stout, strong, spicy, smoky, and you can play around with different combinations of spices to tailor-make it to suit your guest's palate. Great job, Julien!*

Ellipsis

Adapted from a recipe by Devender Sehgal, New Delhi, India.

"I wanted to enhance to flavor of orange in the rum by using both bitter and sweet. Beyond this, I used Taylor's port to compliment the viscosity of the rum. In order to balance these sweet elements I added just a dash of Cynar, creating a well-balanced and delicious cocktail."
—Devender Sehgal.

> 45 ml (1.5 oz) Ron Zacapa 23
> 15 ml (.5 oz) Taylor tawny port
> 10 ml (.33 oz) Cynar
> 1 teaspoon Cointreau
> 2 dashes Angostura bitters
> Stir over ice and strain into a chilled cocktail glass.

gaz sez: *I wrote about this drink in the* San Francisco Chronicle, *and I noted there that, "[The] Ellipsis is very well balanced, indeed, and the Cynar adds a nuance to the drink that makes it stand tall. I really urge you to take this recipe to your local bar and ask the bartender to fix an Ellipsis for you. Lots of bars stock the necessary ingredients." Nicely done, Devender.*

The Emperor

Adapted from a recipe by Valdez Campos, Manifesto, Kansas City, MO.

30 ml (1 oz) Del Maguey Chichicapa Mezcal
30 ml (1 oz) Campari
30 ml (1 oz) dry curaçao
1 orange twist, as garnish

Stir over ice and strain into an old-fashioned glass with a large cube. Add the garnish.

gaz sez: *Wow! I'm stuck for words. So bloody*

Fall Classic

Adapted from a recipe by Bob Brunner, Paragon Restaurant & Bar, Portland, Oregon

Galliano L'Autentico liqueur, as rinse
60ml (2oz) Russell's Reserve 6-year-old rye whiskey

15ml (.5oz) Rothman & Winter Orchard apricot liqueur
15ml (.5oz) Domaine De Canton ginger liqueur
3 dashes Fee Brothers plum bitters
Fresh Plum slice, as garnish

Rinse a chilled cocktail glass with the Galliano; set aside. Stir the remaining ingredients over ice and strain into the glass. Add the garnish.

gaz sez: *Bob Brunner noted that this drink "captures the flavor of Autumn" when he submitted the recipe for his Fall Classic, but I don't really care what time of year it is when I sip this baby. It's a very complex quaff, due mainly to the Galliano L'Autentico, I think, but then again, Russell's Rye is multi-layered in its own right, too. Then there's the plum bitters, made by the one and only Dastardly Joe Fee of Rochester. My hat's off to you again, Joe. Them's a mighty fine bitters, them is.*

53 Souvenirs

Adapted from a recipe by ms. franky marshall, The Dead Rabbit/The Tippler, New York

"53 Souvenirs screams fall and winter and can certainly get you through the colder months, but is also approachable year round. This cocktail is meant to be a shoulder to lean on, a port in a storm, a blanket of warmth to envelope yourself in, perhaps even a crystal ball. Because there's a lot going on in the glass, this is a cocktail made to linger over, escape… to help you remember (or forget). After all, deliciousness has no time limit !"—franky marshall.

45 ml (1.5 oz) Louis Royer Force 53 Cognac
15 ml (.5 oz) Lustau Pedro Ximenez Sherry
4 drops "A L'Olivier" Walnut Oil*
2 Dashes Miracle Mile Chocolate Chili bitters
1 Dash Angostura Bitters
Oil from 1 lemon twist, as an aromatic garnish

Stir over ice and strain into a chilled old-fashioned glass**. Add the garnish, discarding the twist after expressing the oils over the surface of the drink.

Photo: Jennifer Mitchell

*Use a dedicated dropper or sipper straw to add the walnut oil, thus making sure your measurements are correct.

**"You can also serve this over one large ice cube, but personally, i like how this drink changes in the glass as it warms up.– franky marshall.

Large Format:
After pouring out 1 oz Cognac, add 1 oz Walnut Oil to 750 ml Cognac. Let sit for 5-6 hours, agitating once every hour. Strain all through coffee filters to remove excess oil.

gaz sez: *First off I should mention that ms. franky is a personal friend, and a fellow-bartender at New York's Dead Rabbit. That said, I should note that this drink is awesome, and it's made in a style that we don't see too often these days. franky doesn't use smoke and mirrors. There's no caramelized agave syrup smoked with smoldering rooibos tea leaves in this drink. It's a simple affair. My favorite kind of drink.*

Free Rider

Adapted from a recipe by Billy Helmkamp, The Whistler, Chicago, IL.

"I created this drink for February's Mixology Monday, the theme of which was Tiki. Much like the song it was named after, this drink is a mash-up of sorts. It was inspired by two of my favorite cocktails at the moment: Robert Hess' Voyager and Jeffrey Morganthaler's Kingston Club. You can read more about this drink here

30 ml (1 oz) Lemon Hart 151 Demerara rum
30 ml (1 oz) Bénédictine
15 ml (.5 oz) Fernet Branca
45 ml (1.5 oz) pineapple juice
22.5 ml (.75 oz) lime juice
7.5 ml (.25 oz) demerara syrup
2 dashes Angostura bitters
1 mint leaf, as garnish

Shake and strain into a Tiki mug. Fill with crushed ice and add the garnish.

gaz sez: *Oh boy, Oh boy, Oh boy! The combination of Fernet, Bénédictine, and pineapple juice, all lying on a bed of Lemon Hart 151 with pineapple juice sweetening the deal and Angostura jumping in there to make you sit up and take notice is a treat you'll never forget. Billy has sold me on Tiki. Something I never thought would happen.*

The Fruited Pig

Adapted from a recipe by Chad Larson, Cafe Maude at Loring, Minneapolis, MN.

"I was working on my opening cocktail list and I have used this spiced syrup and grapefruit combo before. I wanted to use the Pierre Ferrand 1840 in a cocktail and this seemed like the one I wanted it in. I added the Bittermens bitters and the hops in there kicked the grapefruit notes to a higher level. I was missing something and added the Pig's Nose scotch and that tied the whole thing together. I already have turned several people on to scotch who never really cared for it! It seems like to be a gateway cocktail to enjoy scotch!" —Chad Larson.

45 ml (1.5 oz) Pierre Ferrand 1840 Original Formula cognac
22.5 ml (.75 oz) Pig's Nose scotch whisky
22.5 ml (.75 oz) fresh ruby red grapefruit juice
15 ml (.5 oz) Spiced Tea Syrup*
12 drops Bittermens Hopped Grapefruit bitters
1 grapefruit twist, as garnish

Shake vigorously over ice and strain into a chilled cocktail glass. Squeeze the twist over the drink, then add as garnish.

*Spiced Tea Syrup: Combine 1 teabag of Republic of Tea Cinnamon and Cardamom Tea and 180 ml (6 oz) boiling water in a small saucepan and steep for

30 minutes. Add 200g (1 cup) demerara sugar and heat until sugar dissolves. Cool to room temperature and store in the refrigerator.

gaz sez: *Another hybrid cocktail that calls for two base spirits, cognac and scotch in this case. It's a weird marriage, but it works real well in this case. I think that it's actually the spiced tea syrup that makes it possible for Pierre Ferrand to kiss the Pig's Nose nicely here, and the dozen drops of Bittermens Hopped Grapefruit bitters doesn't go unnoticed, either. Nice work, Chad.*

The Gentlemen's Secret

Adapted from a recipe by Giuseppe Santamaria, Ohla Hotel - Boutique Bar, Barcelona, Spain

Giuseppe Santamaria, Best World Class Bartender Spain 2012, created this drink on occasion of the World Class Final, celebrated in Rio de Janeiro. With "The Gentlemen's Secret" cocktail he won the Hollywood, Bollywood, Hong Kong Challenge, that had to be inspired by stars of the silver screen; a living legend or a screen god or goddess from the past.

He wanted to pay a tribute to the Rat Pack, a group of artists and friends who became a legend in the 60s, for the performances and for living life to full. At the same time, he wanted to play with the romantic idea of bringing them back to the Prohibition Era, where speakeasys spread around. Giuseppe created a delicious twist of the classic cocktail Rob Roy, using a unique blended scotch whisky, Johnny Walker Blue, mixed with some sherry wine PX that gives it a soft and mellow flavour of raisins, and adding a fruity cake flavour of Pear liqueur. The final touch of Lavender bitter releases the chocolate notes of the whisky and add a fresh and relaxing scent note. Perfect as after-dinner.

He managed to surprise some of the most renowned international judges, when he whispered the magic words: "This book contains the secret recipe of the Rat Pack, the "Gentlemen's Secret". They took the book in their hands and… What a surprise!, when they opened it, they found a hip flask hidden in it. Inside it was the cocktail.

Giuseppe Santamaria still keeps surprising his guests at Ohla Boutique Bar, every time he serves this delicious drink.

Note: As an alternative, Johnny Walker Gold can also be used.

40 ml (1.33 oz) Johnny Walker Blue Label scotch
12.5 ml (.42 oz) Pedro Ximenez sherry
15 ml (.5oz) Pear liqueur
5 drops Lavender Bitters
1 lavender flower, as garnish
Stir over ice and strain into a chilled coupette. Add the garnish. (Or present it in a hip flask, hidden in a "Rat Pack book".)

gaz sez: *I'm a sucker for this drink. The flask presentation was fabulous to witness, of course, but like the Rat Pack, it was the drink itself that stole all the limelight. Grear flavors, and great balance.*

The Glorious Socialite

Adapted from a recipe by Benjamin Davies, Oddfellows Chester, Cheshire, UK.

"A well-balanced and spicy aperitif-style drink, loosely based around a dry Manhattan. The majority of these ingredients before you can be found in your Nan's drinks cupboard, which inevitably makes this drink cool." —Benjamin Davies.

35 ml (1.17 oz) Jameson Irish whiskey
20 ml (.66 oz) Aperol
12.5 ml (.42 oz) puerto fino dry sherry
5 ml (.17 oz) Lillet Blanc
1 drop Fee Brothers Whiskey Barrel Aged bitters
1 lemon twist
Shake all ingredients hard and fine-strain into a chilled cocktail glass. Squeeze the twist over the drink, then discard.

gaz sez: *Well, my Nan wasn't much of a one for Aperol, but I think she'd have enjoyed this quaff. There's a bit of a céilidh going on in this glass, but the sherry pulls it all together, making sure that no one gets out of hand. Nice one, Benjamin.*

Golden Prestige

Adapted from a recipe by Nicolas Michel, The bar at the Beau-Rivage Palace, Lausanne, Switzerland.

"My cocktail was created for the Swiss Bacardi Legacy competition, and IT has been selected for the final. Inspired by the legendary daiquiri, I wanted to create a cocktail [that was true to] the roots of Bacardi Superior. A bit of history, a dash of nobility combined with an oriental touch. The idea is to keep the exoticism of the liquid that Don Facundo has bottled 150 years ago and just add a hint of originality," — Nicolas Michel.

50ml (1.7 oz) of Bacardi Superior rum
15ml (.5 ml) fresh passion fruit juice
15ml (.5 ml) of Monin gomme syrup
10ml (.33 ml) of fresh lime juice
1 barspoon orange blossom water*
2 pinches of fresh saffron
1 orange twist, as an aromatic garnish
1 twisted orange zest, as garnish

Shake over ice and fine-strain into a chilled coupette. Perfume the top of the cocktail with the orange twist, and discard. Add the twisted orange zest to the rim of the glass.

*"I just want to let you know that I'm using in my recipe a soft orange blossom water aroma (the brand is Vahiné) and just a bar spoon is enough to get the good balance. So be careful if you use a pure orange blossom water which is going to be stronger... Use maybe the half of a barspoon,"
—Nicolas Michel

gaz sez: *The saffron almost disappears in this drink. But it doesn't disappear. And that's the magic in the Golden Prestige. Well done, sir.*

Good Night Sazerac

Adapted from a recipe by Leonardo Leuci, Jerry Thomas Speakeasy, Rome, Italy.

"This is my personal twist on the classic Sazerac, using two typical Roman ingredients like the chamomile and the Sambuca, and also replacing the Peychaud's with an Italian bitter like Campari." —Leonardo Leuci.

Good Night Sazerac

1 teaspoon sambuca
45 ml (1.5 oz) Evan Williams Black Label bourbon
1 teaspoon homemade chamomile syrup
1 dash Campari
1 dash orange bitters
1 lemon twist, as garnish

Chill an old-fashioned glass by filling with crushed ice. Discard the ice, then add the sambuca to the glass; swirl it around to coat the inside entirely. Discard the excess. Stir the remaining ingredients gently over ice and strain into the prepared glass. Add the garnish.

gaz sez: *Leonardo's using my house bourbon in this one, so he must be a decent lad, right? This is a serious drink. Something that makes you stand up and take notice. It works well with or without the Sambuca rinse, so feel free to try it both ways.*

Grace Note

Adapted from a recipe by Seth Bregman, Bardo Cocktails, Oakland, CA.

"This concoction was created on a warm summer afternoon while trying to figure out interesting things to do with grapefruit. The Aperol and Velvet Falernum work surprisingly well together. The fresh grapefruit binds the ingredients into a pleasantly balanced cocktail, with the peach bitters adding a note of sweetness and complexity to the finish." —Seth Bregman

45 ml (1.5 oz) Stolichnaya, Hangar One,
or Vox Vodka
15 ml (.5 oz) fresh pink grapefruit juice
7.5 ml (.25 oz) Aperol
7.5 ml (.25 oz) Velvet Falernum
2 dashes Fee Bros. Peach Bitters
1 grapefruit twist, as garnish (optional)

Shake over ice and fine-strain into a chilled coupe or cocktail glass. Add the garnish (optional).

gaz sez: *Seth more or less sums up this drink in his comment above. Let e just add that this is the sot of drink that helps us understand just how valuable vodka can be as a base. I tried this recipe with gin, tequila, and white rum. The tequila version was interesting, but the vodka version won the bout hands-down.*

Green Hornet

Adapted from a recipe by Jesper Strauss, ABSURT Cocktails, Copenhagen, Denmark

"I created this cocktail for a summer cocktail competition and actually won. It is fresh and delicious and perfect for a warm summers day. beautiful green colour and the ingredients and colour makes every guest curious about its taste." —Jesper Strauss.

6 sugar-snap peas
8-10 basil leaves
4 slices cucumber
60 ml (2 oz) Tanqueray No. TEN
20 ml (.3 oz) simple syrup
20 ml (.3 oz) fresh lime juice
Cucumber peel, as garnish*

Muddle the cucumber, basil and sugar snaps in a mixing glass. Add the gin, lime juice and simple syrup and shake well. Double strain into a chilled coupe.

*Garnish: Wrap a cucumber peel around your index finger, make a small cut in the middle of the peel and place on the edge of the coupe.

gaz sez: *As a self-confessed commercial tomato-juice hater, it's seldom that I meet a savory-style cocktail that tickles my fancy. This one hits the heights. Springtime in a glass, I think. Great drink.*

Quick Story: *When I received this recipe it called for "sukker snaps," and I thought that it must be some sort of Danish Schnapps so I set to looking for this product. Jesper soon set me straight, and I was off to the market for some sugar-snap peas . . . Duh.*

Gypsy Poem

Adapted from a recipe by Eric Grenier, Honor Kitchen & Cocktails, Emeryville, CA

"A best seller at Honor Kitchen & Cocktails in the winter months." —Eric Grenier

30 ml (1 oz) Laird's Bonded Applejack
30 ml (1 oz) Zacapa 23 Rum
22.5 ml (.75 oz) Averna Amaro
15 ml (.5 oz) fresh lemon juice
15 ml (.5 oz) cinnamon vanilla syrup*

1 barspoon apple butter**
1 dried mini rosebud, as garnish

Shake over ice and fine strain into chilled coupe. Add the garnish.

*Cinnamon Vanilla Syrup In a non-reactive saucepan, over a medium heat, add 1 cup water, 3 cinnamon sticks, and 1 cup demerara sugar. Stir until the sugar is dissolved. Split and scrape one vanilla bean and steep both the bean and seeds in the mixture for 10 minutes. Allow to cool, strain out the solids and bottle. Add a splash of Smith & Cross Navy Strength Rum to bottle to prolong the useful life of the syrup.

**Any fine organic store bought apple butter will suffice, but the end result tastes so much better if you make your own.

gaz sez: *The applejack and Zacapa were made for each other, and the Averna performs the nuptials in this one. Then the syrup adds even more intensity to the drink, and the butter brings a rich, cream texture to the glass. Beautiful.*

Idle Hands

Adapted from a recipe by Payman Bahmani, PDT, New York.

"The aptly named Hellfire Bitters reminded me of the old saying, 'idle hands are the devil's playthings.' This is the devilish creation I came up with when I had some idle time," —Payman Bahmani.

45 ml (1.5 oz) 7 Leguas Reposado tequila
30 ml (1 oz) Anthony Nappa Wines Spezia Gewurztraminer
15 ml (.5 oz) Pierre Ferrand Dry Curacao
7.5 oz (.25 oz) Amaro Averna
2 dashes Bittermen's Hellfire Bitters
Dried chile de arbol, as garnish

Stir over ice and strain into a chilled cocktail coupe. Add the garnish.

gaz sez: *Payman's a real geek when it comes to ingredients, and this was the tamest recipe he submitted this year. This spicy dram comes together beautifully. The Pierre Ferrand Dry Curaçao strides out nicely with the Averno in this one. Nicely done, Payman.*

Inked Zacapa Old Fashioned

Adapted from a recipe by Monica Berg, Aqua Vitae, Oslo, Norway

1 Demerara sugar cube
1 dash squid ink
1 dash Angostura bitters
splash of soda
60 ml (2 oz) Ron Zacapa 23

Place the sugar cube into an old-fashioned glass, and add the squid ink, the bitters, and the club soda. Crush the sugar cube with a barspoon and stir till all is dissolved. Add ice, then add the spirit while stirring constantly.

gaz sez: *This is delectable. The squid ink is hard to detect, but if you search for a slight briny-ness you'll find it here, and the lush sweetness of the Zacapa is the perfect foil!*

Irish Mermaid

Adapted from a recipe by Massimo La Rocca, Ohla Hotel's Boutique Bar, Barcelona, Spain.

"The name Mermaid refers to the statue of the little Mermaid in Copenhagen, which is where this great cherry liqueur comes from. When I created this drink, the bar I was working at was very famous for afternoon tea. I wanted to start selling cocktails during those hours, so I decided to throw this drink right at the customers' tables with a crystal teapot so that people would get curious about cocktails.

"The drink showcases the warmth of the beautiful Irish whiskey with the slight bitterness of the Aperol, perfectly balanced by the combination of cherry and almond flavours. Angostura gives it a nice depth, while the orange twist provides nice and fresh citrus notes to the cocktail." —Massimo La Rocca.

35 ml (1.17 oz) quality Irish whiskey
10 ml (.33 oz) Cherry Heering
10 ml (.33 oz) Aperol
5 ml (.17 oz) orgeat syrup
2 dashes Angostura bitters
1 orange twist, as garnish
1 barspoon brandied black cherries,
cooked and reduced in Cherry Heering,
as garnish

Combine in a glass or crystal teapot and throw to create a beautiful froth. Strain into a chilled coupe and add the garnishes.

gaz sez: *Superb! The Aperol and orgeat dance together all night in your mouth after drinking just one of these babies. Max: It's almost like you know what you're doing!*

Jack Jazz Rabbit

Adapted from a recipe by Marek Vojcarcik, U.N.C.L.E., Bangkok, Thailand

"I think that many people will enjoy my Jack Jazz Rabbit, especially in summer time.

[The] recipe is twist on my grandmother's salad which she used to serve me during my childhood at late afternoons :-) It brings me always nice memories. The name comes from an old PC game where the hero is really crazy Rabbit who always messes around and collects carrots. [The flavor] is very fruity, natural and it's a combination of healthy ingredients that will maybe very interesting for many people :-). The cocktail was first prepared for Bar Amazement Competition by Stan Vadrna and was served for more than half a year in Bratislava," —Marek Vojcarcik

1/4 granny smith apple, cut into small cubes
20ml (.6 oz) fresh lemon juice
20ml (.6 oz) gomme sirop
80ml (2.4 oz) fresh carrot juice
40ml (1.3 oz) Zubrowka or Smirnoff apple vodka
Fresh carrot sticks(rabbit ears) and apple fan, as garnishes

Muddle the apple in a mixing glass, add ice and the rest of the ingredients, and shake well. Strain into an ice-filled collins glass, and add the garnishes.

gaz sez: *If you know my taste in cocktails you'll no doubt be aware that this is not they style of drink I usually favor, but this recipe pretty much intrigued me so I had to give it a chance. Guess what? It's fabulous. And it's so unlike the vast majority of recipes that usually cross my desk, so I just had to choose it as one of this year's winners. There's chance I'll be in Bangkok next year, and if that comes true, I'll go pay Marek a visit for sure.*

Jake Barnes

Adapted from a recipe by Natalie Jacob, Dutch Kills, Long Island City, NY.

"The Jack Rose has always been one of my favorite classic cocktails, and Lairds one of my favorite spirit brands. It is so rich in history, and not only history of our great spirits industry, but rich in history of our country and my home state New Jersey. My other favorite classic cocktail containing Lairds was the Jack in the box aka Jersey City. This cocktail is featured in David Embury's The Fine Art of Mixing Drinks under cocktails based on the applejack sour. Which is what really comes to mind when I think of a jack rose, sweet and sour and strong. I am also born and raised in Jersey City, and I thought it would be fun to [make a variation] on both cocktails together.

" I wanted to smooth it out a little more and the sweetness of the pineapple juice takes care of that, and the lemon juice balances it out from making it too sweet, grenadine (because it wouldn't be a jack rose without it), Lairds Applejack, and a dash of angostura bitters to add more depth to the drink. Quite simple, but I believe some of the best cocktails are.

"I named it after the character in Ernest Hemingway's novel, the Sun Also Rises, because Jake Barnes sits down at the bar of the Paris Crillon Hotel and orders a Jack Rose." —Natalie Jacob

45 ml (1.5 oz) Laird's applejack
15 ml (.5 oz) ounce fresh lemon juice
15 ml (.5 oz) fresh pineapple juice
3/4 ounce grenadine
1 dash Angostura bitters
1 pineapple wedge, as garnish

Shake over ice and strain into a chilled coupe. Add the garnish.

gaz sez: *I wrote about this one in the San Francisco Chronicle, and I totally agree with Natalie when she says, "Quite simple, but I believe some of the best cocktails are."*

Jake Leg

Adapted from a recipe by Dimitris Kiakos, Bartender/owner at the Gin Joint, Athens, Greece

60 ml (2 oz) Beefeater 24 London dry Gin
10 ml (.3 oz) Storico Vermouth di Torino
20 ml (.6 oz) fresh lemon juice
15 ml (.5 oz) pine honey syrup*
10 ml (.3 oz) homemade ginger syrup**
25 ml (.85 oz) sage tea***
2 dashes Dr. Adam Elmegirab's Boker's bitters
1 sage leaf, as garnish

Shake over ice and strain into a chilled coupe. Add the garnish

***Pine Honey Syrup:** blend 500 ml (2 cups) Greek pine honey with 300 ml (1.25 cups) simple syrup.

****Homemade Ginger Syrup:** blend 500 ml (2 cups) freshly squeezed ginger juice with 500 ml (2 cups) simple syrup

*****Sage Tea:** boil in a saucepan 500 ml (2 cups) water with 15 sage leaves for 8 minutes. Remove from heat and strain.

gaz sez: *Dimitris really captured the essence of Beefeater 24 in this drink, especially with his sage tea—it marries fabulously with the gin. Nicely done, Dimitris.*

Jenkins!

Adapted from a recipe by Kate McDonald, Veneto Lounge, Victoria, BC.

"When I started bartending I was eager to make my own drink, but patience is necessary both for great things and product conservation. This was the first drink I created (with the newly acquired knowledge of flavour affinities), and years later it still seems to be the number one drink my patrons order and tell their friends about.

"Yes, the name is supposed to have an exclamation mark. The chef I was working with at the time use to call me Jenkins. At first I simply thought he didn't know my name, but I think he just liked to yell that more than 'Katie.' The name has now become a sort of 'nom-de-bar' used by those who have worked with me." —Kate McDonald.

60 ml (2 oz) Hendrick's gin
22.5 ml (.75 oz) Giffard Lichi Li liqueur
22.5 ml (.75 oz) fresh lemon juice
15 ml (.5 oz) honey syrup
7.5 ml (.25 oz) rose water
1 dash Bitter Truth lemon bitters

Shake and double-strain into chilled coupe.

gaz sez: *Pure, simple, refreshing, and perfect for springtime sipping. This drink will fly over the bar at a very rapid rate of knots.*

La Croix Elixir

Adapted from a recipe by Humberto Marques, 1105 Cocktail Bar, Copenhagen, Denmark.

"The motto of the Carthusian monks is **Stat crux dum volvitur orbis**, which is latin for "The Cross is steady while the world is turning." Like the monks motto, the world is turning, while this drink is steady. It has a special blend of two herbal liqueurs, also made by monks from a secret recipe.

"A truly apothecary and sour style cocktail where herbs and spices are pairing perfectly together. These herbs and spices add to the fresh and floral G'Vine gin. The citrus notes of fresh lime, pineapple syrup and pineapple sage balances overall the cocktail. To top it off the addition egg whites gives a silky smooth taste sensation.

"La Croix Elixir will make your world spin."

60 ml (2 oz) G'Vine gin
15 ml (.5 oz) Green Chartreuse
15 ml (.5 oz) Bénédictine
4 Pineapple sage leafs
30 ml (1 oz) Pineapple syrup
30 ml (1 oz) fresh lime juice
1 dash of egg white
2 drops of chocolate bitters
1 pineapple-sage sprig, as garnish.

Dry shake; shake again over ice, and strain into a small chilled wine goblet. Add the garnish.

gaz sez: *It took balls to use both Chartreuse and Bénédictine in the same glass, and though I've seen this done before, I've never seen it pulled off quite so elegantly. Perhaps it's the G'Vine that pulls everything together? And the sage leaves don't hurt, either. Another nice one, Humberto!*

The Last Wynd

Adapted from a recipe by Sian Ferguson, 99 Bar and Kitchen, Aberdeen, Scotland.

"Twist on a Last Word, made for the 'Who will have the last word' competition in the UK. Winner of the Aberdeen round. Awaiting other cities winners to see who will win over all." —Sian Ferguson.

25 ml (.83 oz) Havana Club 3 Años rum
25 ml (.83 oz) yellow Chartreuse
25 ml (.83 oz) maraschino liqueur

25 ml (.83 oz) fresh lime juice
1 barspoon honey
Shake over ice and double-strain into a chilled coupette.

gaz sez: *Try this. Run, don't walk. The Chartreuse and the maraschino bang out a beautiful duet in this baby, and the rum provides a sturdy stage for them. Promise.*

Leaving Manhattan

Adapted from a recipe by Joanne Spiegel, Mercury Bar West, New York City.

"Leaving Manhattan, as you know, won first place in the final for the Woodford Reserve Manhattan Experience. The challenge was to enhance or contrast the existing flavors and notes of Woodford Reserve. It being a cold winter's day when I pondered on this, I thought touching on chocolate and wood notes would be a good place to start. I felt the use of Punt E Mes would add to the sweetness but would also bring enough bittering elements that once combined with the bittering elements of the orange bitters I would achieve an intriguing balance—plus I read somewhere that Italians love drinking the stuff when eating dark chocolate so in it went!

"For the garnish I had found the dark chocolate stir sticks in a tea house and I thought with the use of the tea syrup and the chocolate already this a perfect fun garnish—the orange spiral added a pop of much needed color and personally I can't get enough orange essence and oils when I sip bourbon." —Joanne Spiegel.

60 ml (2 oz) Woodford Reserve bourbon
15 ml (.5 oz) Punt E Mes
7.5 ml (.25 oz) dark crème de cacao
7.5 ml (.25 oz) Lapsang Smoked Tea Syrup*
2 dashes orange bitters

1 chocolate or orange flavored stir stick
wrapped with orange spiral**
Stir over ice and strain into a chilled
coupe. Add the garnish.

JOANN SPIEGEL
LEAVING MANHATTAN

* For the Lapsang smoked tea syrup, combine 4 ounces hot strong lapsang souchong tea and 1/2 cup granulated sugar; stir to dissolve the sugar. Let cool to room temperature before using. Refrigerate leftovers.

**When preparing garnish, peel orange spiral next to glass so essential oils spray over glass and cocktail. Wrap spiral around chocolate stick and rest garnish on the lip of the glass off to one side.

Note: *Bartenders from sixteen cities across the country came to The Dream Hotel in New York City to show off their twist on the Manhattan cocktail at the Woodford Reserve Manhattan Experience, an event presented by Woodford along with Esquire magazine, and it was New York bartender Joanne Spiegel of Mercury Bar West that took top honors. gaz was a judge at this event, along with David Wondrich, Leo Robitschek of Eleven Madison Park, and Chris Morris, Master Distiller for Woodford Reserve.*

gaz sez: *I wrote about this drink in the* San Francisco Chronicle, *and I was amused to see the following comment from a reader: I might order it in a bar, but to make this at home? Nah. I am not going to galavant all over Clement St. looking for some obscure tea to make some syrup. Now I'm the first to admit that some cocktail recipes have gotten a bit out of control of late, but to think of Lapsang Souchong tea as being too exotic brought a smile to my face. Look in your local bloody supermarket, man! Joanne did a fabulous job with this drink, and she deserves a round of applause. Let's hear it for Joanne Spiegel!*

Liberty Flip

Adapted from a recipe by Leo Lahti, Pustervik, Göteborg, Sweden

"This was created for the Bacardi Legacy Cocktail Competetion and has reached the final stage of the Swedish competition. It is a twist on the Cuba Libre, with both a modern twist and a nod to the early years of drinking." —Leo Lahti

50 ml (1.7 oz) Bacardi Superior
10 ml (.3 oz) Swedish Punsch
25 ml (.85) Coca Cola & lime reduction
5 ml (.2 oz) simple syrup
1 egg
Nutmeg, as garnish

Combine all ingredients in a shaker and dry shake for about 15 seconds. Then shake with cubed ice for another 15 seconds or so and fine strain in a chilled champagne flute. Grate a little nutmeg on top.

Coca Cola & Lime Reduction Bring 330 ml (11 oz) of Coca-Cola to a boil and then let it simmer until it has been reduced to approximately 100 ml (3.4 oz). Then add 20 ml of lime juice and 20 ml of simple syrup.

gaz sez: *This is a weird bird, indeed, but it's a very friendly drink, and I love seeing people who know how to work with Swedish Punsch, the ingredient that peeks out from under the Coca Cola lime reduction here to make sure nobody forgets about it. Nicely done, Leo.*

McMillian

Adapted from a recipe by Geoffrey Wilson, Loa, New Orleans, LA.

"Made on Chris McMillian's birthday using all ingredients that he's used in his cocktails. I know, I know. I promise not to name anything else after him and start naming cocktails after Laura now. But I guess it's a tribute to both of 'em and how they welcomed my family into their family." —Geoffrey Wilson.

60 ml (2 oz) Rittenhouse rye whiskey
15 ml (.5 oz) orange curacao
15 ml (.5 oz) orgeat syrup
7.5 ml (.25 oz) Bénédictine
7.5 ml (.25 oz) fresh lemon juice
1 dash Angostura bitters
5 mint leaves (reserve 1 for garnish)

Shake over ice and strain into a chilled glass (use a strainer and tea strainer). Add the garnish.

gaz sez: *Raindrops on roses, and whiskers on kittens, are, for sure, a few of my favorite things. They rank alongside Rittenhouse Rye, Bénédictine, and Angostura bitters, so this baby grabbed my attention immediately I saw it. Chris McMillian: Your namesake cocktail ain't too shabby at all! Nicely done, Geoffrey.*

The Merriweather Old-Fashioned

Adapted from a recipe by René Kronsteiner, Sea Cloud Cruises, Hamburg, Germany

"This is Sea Cloud Cruises' signature drink—a tribute to the late Marjorie Merriweather Post Hutton the original owner of the 4-masted Sea Cloud, the famed 1930 luxury yacht still operated today. Linie Aquavit is used because it crosses the Equator twice on a vessel before being bottled, and the orange bitters are a reference to Hutton´s famed winter retreat Mar-a-Lago in Florida. The Maldon sea salt is frequently used on board Sea Cloud by our chefs and the Sailmaker's needle, well.... 'cause it's a real square rigged ship with traditional sails . This is a chameleon like drink that spikes off with a zesty tang and if [left to] sit [for a while it] turns into a soothing flavourful drink as the ice and the sea salt melt."
—René Kronsteiner.

50 ml (1.7 oz) Linie Aquavit
1 bar spoon Campari
1 lump of Sugar
1 bar spoon The Bitter Truth Orange Bitters
1 splash water
1 pinch of Maldon sea salt
1 long strip of orange zest
1 Sailmakers needle Size 10

Methodology: In an old-fashioned glass, saturate the lump of sugar with orange bitters, then add a splash of water to dissolve(use a pestle). Fill the glass with ice cubes and add well chilled Linie Aquavit and Campari. Stir briskly,and sprinkle the Maldon Sea Salt on top. Serve with a long orange zest on the Sailmaker's needle.

gaz sez: *Brilliant. Just brilliant.*

Milord Gower

Adapted from a recipe by Frederic Yarm, Cocktail Virgin Blog, Somerville, MA.

"St. Germaine [cocktail] appears in the 1937 Café Royal Cocktail Book, it pre-dates the elderflower liqueur of the same name by over 70 years, and it features a healthy slug of green Chartreuse that helped it get its name. The name is a reference to the Comte de St. Germaine who claimed to have created the Elixir of Life; Chartreuse was referred to as an elixir of life as well, although the two elixirs were unrelated until the creation of this recipe. In my variation, I swapped the original's green Chartreuse, grapefruit, lemon, and mint garnish for yellow Chartreuse, orange, lime, and orange bitters garnish but kept the egg white-sour base the same. For a name, I went with Milord Gower, who was a Parisian comedian that made making fun of St. Germaine's grand claims and far-fetched stories a large part of his act. The resultant cocktail is rather ambrosial and easy to drink." —Frederic Yarm.

45 ml (1.5 oz) yellow Chartreuse
22.5 ml (.75 oz) fresh orange juice
22.5 ml (.75 oz) fresh lime juice
1 egg white
5 drops orange bitters, as garnish

Dry-shake, then add ice. Shake again and strain into a chilled cocktail glass. Add the garnish.

gaz sez: *What a weird damned drink! But what a fabulous story, huh? "Get into the bar business and your education will be complete," said my Dad. You were right again, Bernard. And this drink, weird as it might be, is worth a spin or two around the block. Try it and tell me I'm wrong.*

Minty Silk

Adapted from a recipe by Diana Haider, The Parlour, Frankfurt am Main, Deutschland

3 barspoons of homemade lemon curd*
about 6 mintleaves
40 ml (1.33 oz) gin
15 ml (.5 oz) sugar
15 ml (.5 oz)fresh lemon juice
30 ml (1 oz) fresh orange juice
1 small edible flower, sprinkled with gold dust, as garnish.

Shake (hard) over ice and double strain into a double old-fashioned glass filled with one

*Lemon Curd
50 grams (2 oz) unsalted butter
110 (4 oz) granulated sugar
pinch of salt
2 eggs
1 egg yolk
juice and zest of 2 lemons

Melt the butter over a low heat, add the sugar, salt, lemon juice and the zests Beat the eggs, add them to the other ingredients, and stir constantly with a wooden spoon until it gets velvety & thick. Remove from the heat, allow to cool, and refrigerate.

gaz sez: *Okay, I cheated and used commercial lemon curd when I tested this one, but it was a really fine brand. Honest. Jared Brown and Anistatia Miller were the fine folk who told me about this drink—I think they sampled it at Diana's bar in Germany, and let me tell you this: If I see a recipe that calls for both gin and lemon curd, it's sure as hell going to get my attention. This drink is nothing short of a masterpiece. Well done, Diana.*

Mont Blanc Cocktail

Adapted from a recipe by Lee Morris, The Alchemist, Leeds, UK

"I created this cocktail for the 2013 Masters of Maraschino competition. The name refers to the use of both French and Italian ingredients in the drink. The Mont Blanc tunnel, of course, being a physical link between the two countries," —Lee Morris.

45ml (1.5 oz) dried-apricot-infused Remy Martin VSOP cognac
15ml (.5 oz) Luxardo maraschino
15ml (.5 oz) Cocci Americano
1 dash Fee Brothers Whiskey-Barrel-Aged Bitters
1 dash Regans' Orange Bitters No.6
Burnt Chartreuse rinse

Flame a cocktail glass with Green Chartreuse sprayed from an atomizer. Stir the remaining ingredients over ice and strain into the glass.

gaz sez: *I infused a cup of dried apricots into 750-ml of cognac to make this one, and although it wasn't specified, I used green Chartreuse, as is my wont. The whole thing came together beautifully with the Burnt Chartreuse rinse playing a far bigger role in this opera than I'd have guessed.*

Myrrah's Passion

Adapted from a recipe by Lindsay Laubenstein, Enoteca Emilia, Cincinnati, OH

37.5 ml (1.25 oz) Buffalo Trace bourbon
15 ml (.5 oz) crème de violette
22.5 ml (.75 oz) fresh lemon juice
7.5 ml (.25 oz) simple syrup (made at 2:1 sugar/water ratio)
egg-white foam*
2 dashes Aphrodite Bitters, as an aromatic garnish

Shake the bourbon, crème de violette, lemon juice, and simple syrup over ice, and strain into a chilled cocktail glass. Top with egg white foam and the Aphrodite Bitters.

*Egg-white Foam
In a clean shaker, dry shake an egg white until a bit frothy. Add 1/2 tsp granulated or superfine sugar to shaker and continue to dry shake until desired density is achieved.

gaz sez: *Aphrodite Bitters, by the by, are a "unique, hand-crafted cocktail ingredient" from Dr. Adam Elmegirab which take their name from the Greek goddess of sexuality and love. According to Adam, "The finest chocolate, cocoa nibs, ginger root, red chilli, Arabica coffee and ginseng are compounded to create a complex flavour profile with each botanical playing off and enhancing one another, when these bitters are made. No matter* what Adam says, though, take it from me that these bitters work perfectly as an aromatic garnish. And I'm a sucker for a good aromatic garnish.

Beneath the garnish, though, you'll find an intriguing cocktail wherein the Buffalo Trace is itching to play around with the crème de violette, and he succeeds, too, but the lemon juice and simple syrup are in the glass, too, so the whiskey reigns himself in a little to give them some space. Great compromise.

Negrita

Adapted from a recipe by Giuseppe Gallo, Purple Bar at Sanderson Hotel, London, UK.

30 ml (1 oz) Tequila Ocho plata
20 ml (.66 oz) Campari
20 ml (.66 oz) Barolo Chinato wine
1 lime twist, as garnish
1 cucumber slice, as garnish

Stir over ice and strain into a rocks glass over an ice chunk. Add the garnishes.

gaz sez: *Repeat after me: Tequila Ocho is incredible; Tequila Ocho is incredible; Tequila Ocho is incredible. And when you combine it with the incomparable Campari and the multi-dimensional Barolo Chinato (macerated with over 20 ingredients including cardamom, calisaya, gentian, and citrus peels), you just can't go wrong. Bravo, Giuseppe Gallo!*

The New Fashioned Old Fashioned

Adapted from a recipe by Jens Kerger, Pinta Cocktailbar, Dresden, Germany

"To me, the Four Roses Single Barrel bourbon is a great choice for something as simple as the Old Fashioned. It carries loads of character, all of which are underlined by this choice of ingredients. Bitter Orange Marmalade goes well with almost any kind of Bourbon, ripe for experimentation. Plum Jam also is a great addition to the fruity notes of this whiskey—in that case kick the orange twist and drop in a Cognac soaked plum, if you can find one. The Cinnamon together with the bitters compliments the fine wooden notes, lending a subtle first impression by flavor, and adding to the already deep complexity.

"There's also been a twist to the twist already. Natalie (bar owner of Mojo Record Bar, Sydney) omitted the powdered sugar and the Chocolate Bitters and used 10ml Mozart Dry Chocoloate Liqueur. Also, if you think this drink is still not complex enough and needs an extra kick, drop 5 dried cloves in before shaking," —Jens Kerger

60ml (2 oz) Four Roses Single Barrel Bourbon
2 teaspoons Olde English Orange Marmalade
1 to 1.5 teaspoons powdered sugar*
1 dash Mozart Dry Chocolate Bitters (or mole bitters)

1 dash Jerry Thomas' Own Decanter
Bitters (or Boker's or Peychaud's)
1 stick of cinnamon

Light the cinnamon stick and catch the smoke in a tumbler. In a shaker, add all ingredients except the cinnamon. Add some ice and shake the hell out of it. Double strain over ice ball or large format cube in the pre-cinnamon smoked tumbler. Add the cinnamon stick (burnt side down) and a huge orange zest.

gaz sez: *I used castor sugar (1 teaspoon) rather than powdered sugar, but other than that, even though Jens offered lots of* *suggestions for variations, I stuck to the original formula. It was fabulous. I loves me some orange marmalade, I does. I'll be serving these to friends tonight!*

Norwegian Negroni

Adapted from a recipe by Adam Harness, Cafe Maude, Minneapolis, MN.

"A very light and herbal/citrus taste, perfect for a before dinner libation. Due to the fact that many Minnesotans are of Norwegian heritage, I thought this would be a good starter for someone who wants to experience a craft cocktail." —Adam Harness.

60 ml (2 oz) Linie aquavit
22.5 ml (.75 oz) Noilly Prat dry vermouth
22.5 ml (.75 oz) Aperol
2 dashes Bittercube orange bitters
1 lemon twist, as garnish

Stir over ice and strain over an ice chunk in a low-ball glass. Add the garnish.

gaz sez: *This is a delightful use of aquavit. The drink is simple, dry, and very sophisticated. One of my favorites this year.*

Norwegian Sour

Adapted from a recipe by Katrin Reitz, La Dee Da, Bad Honnef Am Rhein, Nordrhein-Westfalen, Germany.

"In and around Bad Honnef and surroundings my bar La Dee Da is also called "The Norwegian Bar" because my partner is from Norway. Hence we needed a fitting cocktail for the nickname. Aquavit is a challenging ingredient because of its intensity, but this cocktail makes me proud because it balances the strong notes of the linie with spices and floral notes perfectly." —Katrin Reitz

40 ml (1.3 oz) Linie Aquavit
10 ml (.3 oz) St. Germain Elderflower Liquor
20 ml (.6 oz) Arabian Spice Syrup*
20 ml (.6 oz) fresh lemon juice

Shake over ice and fine strain into a chilled coupe. . Serve without extra garnish on a silver coaster.

*Arabian Spice Syrup
Simmer 200grams (7 ounces) of white sugar and two tablespoons of Ras el Hasun Spice mix in 200ml (7 ounces) of water for 2 minutes. Strain through a fine sieve, and refrigerate.

Ras el Hanout Recipe by Hassan McSouli, Taken From http://www.sbs.com.au/

Ras el hanout, which translates literally as "head of the shop", originated in the Meghribi villages of North Africa. It is a complex and distinctive mix of about 20 to 27 spices and herbs, the quantities of which vary according to the maker. Specific quantities are a much guarded secret from one spice shop to the next, and blending is considered an art. Ras el hanout is used with poultry, meat, game, rice and couscous. It can be found already mixed, like in specialty stores. If you are unable to find it, here is a simple recipe for you to make your own.

1 1/2 tsp black peppercorns
1 tsp ground ginger
1 tsp cumin seeds
1 tsp coriander seeds
1 tsp ground cinnamon
1/2 tsp ground nutmeg 1/2 tsp cardamom seeds
1/2 tsp hot paprika
4 whole cloves
1/2 tsp ground turmeric
1/2 tsp sea salt
1/2 tsp ground allspice

Grind all ingredients together with a mortar and pessle.

gaz sez: *Thanks, Katrin (a bartender who I met at the 2013 finals of G'Vine's Gin Connoisseur Program), for turning me* *onto Ras el hanout—it was readily available on Amazon, and I now use your Arabian Spice Syrup to give an extra little kick to my third cup of coffee almost every day. Takes the edge off that microwave bitterness. Thanks also for your kick-ass cocktail recipe! The Norwegian Sour is one of those drinks that's astounding at first taste, and comforting through the whole coupe-full. Well done!*

Not Coming Home

Adapted from a recipe by Tim Rabior, Oddfellows, Miami Beach

"I came up with this one while working at Sanctuaria in St. Louis. I was on an absinthe kick and was trying to make cocktails with it that were more palatable to the common consumer than just absinthe, sugar and water. The name comes from lyrics in Every Time I Die's song **White Smoke**, though I found it applicable to this drink as well."—Tim Rabior

45 ml (1.5 oz) Dolin Blanc
22.5 ml (.75 oz) St. George absinthe .
22.5 ml (.75 oz) St Germaine
4 Dashes Cortas Orange Flower Water
1 grapefruit twist, as garnish

Stir over ice and strain into a chilled cocktail glass. Add the garnish.

gaz sez: *Absolutely brilliant use of absinthe here. Brilliant. It's there, but it plays nice with its friends in the Not Coming Home. Very impressive.*

Old Fashioned No. 6

Adapted from a recipe by Oron Lerner, Mapal Bar, Haifa, Israel.

"I did this for TotC's Truly Old Fashioned entry, which is sadly the only one open to any bartenders and not just US ones. I sent this recipe for an Old Fashioned contest and was looking for a way to create something modern, new and still true to the Old Fashioned.

"I recently tried and enjoyed Guiseppe Gonzalez's Trinidad Sour, using 1.5 oz of Angostura Aromatic Bitters, and the guests around here have recently found the Seelbach cocktail to be very pleasing so I decided to try and reverse the ratios in an Old Fashioned and create a recipe that uses bitters by the ounces. Yours was first on the list and sampling the bitters straight, I came up with the recipe. The cognac rounds the flavors, the sweetness balances the bitters and the smoky flavor adds a pop to the drink. Looking for a fitting garnish I found a jar of Bergamot peels infusing and gave it a try, which added perfumy scents and it just ended up splendid.

"I currently run the Mapal bar. Mapal is an abbreviation of 'waterfall,' but could also be short for 'Word of Mouth,' which is exactly what it is, a very small (20 seat), quiet bar, focusing on providing a cocktail atmosphere at reasonable prices. We are a speakeasy styled bar, so no address and no publicity, but we occasionally do open cocktail nights in other bars and are usually a great success, by local standards of course." —Oron Lerner.

30 ml (1 oz) Regans' Orange Bitters No. 6
30 ml (1 oz) V.S. cognac
22.5 ml (.75 oz) Demerara & Smoked Tea Syrup*
1 orange twist, as garnish

Build in an old-fashioned glass over a large chunk of ice. Add the garnish.

***Demerara & Smoked Tea Syrup:**
Combine 200 g (1 cup) demerara sugar, 240 ml (1 cup) water, and 1 tablespoon smoked tea leaves (I use Du Tigre, but any other variety such as Lapsang Souchong can be used) in a saucepan. Dissolve sugar in water and continue cooking until almost boiling. Filter, let cool, and bottle.

gaz sez: *I know young Oron from the G'Vine Gin Connoisseur Program, and I can vouch for the fact that he's a great sport, and a fabulous bartender, too. This guy is one of the few bartenders who has been experimenting with using large amounts of bitters in their new creations, and he's got a good handle on how to make this work. I think that it's Oron's Demerara & Smoked Tea Syrup that binds this one together and gives it a sturdy backbone, though. It's a very well-constructed drink.*

Old Fashioned (Red House Style)

Adapted from a recipe created at Red House, Paris

"This is our house old fashioned, and it's a killer. We have probably attained the world record for most Pimento Dram and Drambuie consumed by any bar in the world, (along with cynar and picon - but that's another story.)" —Joe Boley

40 ml (1.3 oz) Jim Beam Rye
10 ml (.3 oz) Bitter Truth Pimento Dram
1 cl. Drambuie
1 cardamom pod
1 lemon twist, as garnish
1 orange twist, as garnish

Muddle the Cardamom pod in a mixing glass. Add ice and the remaining ingredients, stir, and fine strain over a big ice ball. Add the garnishes.

gaz sez: *Killer is, indeed, what this drink is all about. Jeez, Looeez it fair does the Tango all over your mouth with spices running, jumping, and landing gracefully every single time. Run to the Red House and tell the crew I sent you. Then tip real big. Okay?*

Old Quartermaster

Adapted from a recipe by Michael Shea, Rum Club, Portland, OR

"Last November we were enjoying Manhattans at Rum Club made with Pampero Anniversario and PX sherry. I wanted to put the drink on the menu, but it had to be adapted so it wasn't a $14 cocktail. I took my cue from an old Trader Vic's recipe for a drink that we featured on our opening menu, the Quarterdeck Cocktail: Gosling's rum, modified by a touch of blended scotch and cream sherry.

"The name come from a regular who often ordered the drink. He spent time enlisted in the Coast Guard as a Quartermaster, so we have a Quarterdeck Cocktail for an old Quartermaster!" —Michael Shea.

30 ml (1 oz) Mt. Gay Eclipse Black rum
22.5 ml (.75 oz) Famous Grouse scotch whisky
15 ml (.5 oz) Pedro Ximenez sherry
4 drops smoky scotch (Ardbeg, Caol Ila), as garnish
1 orange twist, as garnish

Stir over ice and strain into a small chilled cocktail glass or coupe. Add the garnish so that each drop represents a point of a compass. Squeeze the twist over the drink, then discard.

gaz sez: *This is one of those drinks that really shouldn't work, but it does. The sherry brings everything together in harmony in this one, and I love the aromatic garnishes. Nice.*

Papa Needs a New Pair of Shoes

Adapted from a recipe by Patrick Halloran, The Belcourt Theatre, Nashville, TN.

"Christened by a coworker's girlfriend who, upon smelling the rinse, said the drink smelled like a shoe.

"The Belcourt Theatre is one of the oldest independently owned movie theatres in the South, and it is the only such theatre in Nashville. We specialize in foreign, independent, arthouse and repertory cinema, 99% of which we still project in 35mm instead of digital. While perhaps not a bar in the strictest definition, we have a "full" bar which I've spent the last two years trying to improve. It is a slow and uphill battle, but I'm trying. Drinks like this, while simple, are starting to get customers in the habit of asking for something beyond a Jack and Coke.

"Since the ingredients are so simple, I searched up and down to make sure I didn't accidentally invent someone else's drink before I submitted this. The only one that came close was from the Washington Square Tavern which uses Overholt, Fernet, and demerara. Coincidentally the drink is called the Feet First! Apparently those three ingredients invoke feet to bartenders?"—Patrick Halloran.

45 ml (1.5 oz) Old Overholt rye whiskey
15 ml (.5 oz) Fernet Branca
15 ml (.5 oz) 2:1 demerara syrup
22.5 ml (.75 oz) fresh lemon juice
14 drops Fee Brothers Old Fashion bitters
Laphroaig scotch whisky (for rinse)

Shake vigorously over ice and double-strain into a chilled coupe that has been rinsed with Laphroaig.

gaz sez: *Hmm ... Feet, huh? I always thought that Laphroaig—which I happen to adore—smelled more like a 3rd-*

world clinic filled with cigar smoke. Each to his own, I guess. I confess to using Bulleitt rye when I tested this drink, and there's quite a difference between Bulleitt and Overholt, but what the hell. This is my style of drink. I love it. Simple as that.

Paradise Punch

Adapted from a recipe by Cynthia Turner, Imperial Life, Asheville, North Carolina

"We recently featured this on our cocktail menu with a house made falernum, but for this recipe I chose the widely distributed Velvet Falernum so anyone can enjoy. I love the exotic flavors the arrack contributes. I hope you enjoy it, gaz,"
—Cynthia Turner.

30 ml (1 oz) Ransom Old Tom gin
22.5 ml (.75 oz) Batavia Arrack
15 ml (.5 oz) Velvet Falernum
15 ml (.5 oz) Cherry Heering
22.5 ml (.75 oz) fresh orange juice
15 ml (.5 oz) fresh lime juice
Splash soda water
Grated nutmeg and a lime wheel, as garnishes

Shake all ingredients except for the soda over ice. Strain over fresh ice in a Collins glass, top with the soda and stir briefly. Add the garnishes.

gaz sez: *Did I like it, Cynthia? I loved it! Very funky, indeed. It's as if the Old Tom and the arrack were made for each other, and the falernum is officiating at the union. Tres kewl, indeed.*

Patriarch

Adapted from a recipe by Daniel Brancusi, Vitae, New York City.

67.5 ml (2.25 oz) Rittenhouse rye whiskey
15 ml (.5 oz) Luxardo maraschino liqueur
10 ml (.33 oz) English Bishop*
1 dash Angostura bitters
1 dash orange bitters
1 large orange twist, as garnish

Stir over ice and strain into a chilled coupe. Add the garnish.

*English Bishop:

Stud an orange with about 40 cloves and bake at 205 degrees C (400 degrees F) until golden brown. Quarter the orange and place in a saucepan with 750 ml of port. Simmer for 20 minutes and then add about 200 g (1 cup) of sugar. Cool and bottle.

gaz sez: *I'd never made English Bishop before testing this recipe, and I'm here to tell you I'll be making it again. After testing this cocktail a couple of times, and deciding it's one of the best new drinks I've tasted this year, I added cognac to the remaining Bishop—50:50 ratio—and sipped it for a nightcap when I felt I deserved it. Okay, I sipped it every night till it was all gone . . . Nice one, Daniel!*

Perfect Tickler

Adapted from a recipe by Carol Donovan, Intoxicatingly Fun Cocktails, Chicago, IL.

"I tried this with different flowers, and liked it with lavender, but the rose allowed for a beautiful glittery garnish! (I edge rose petals with edible glitter and float them on top). With the different flowers I had to tweak the ratios. The apple is really the only weight in the cocktail at all, so it needs to be muddled fairly well to extract fibers and juice both.

For batching, I did use rose water rather than trying to get enough of the rose from petals.

"This drink was a finalist in the Paris of the Plains cocktail competition 2012, and in the spirit of the fun I stirred it with a French tickler for the judging. :) It was universally well received by attendees and I am proud of how it turned out." —Carol Donovan.

1/3 Granny Smith apple, sliced
6 edible rose petals (reserve 1 for garnish)
45 ml (1.5 oz) Plymouth gin
15 ml (.5 oz) St. Germaine
15 ml (.5 oz) Cocchi Americano
15 ml (.5 oz) fresh lime juice
1 drop absinthe, as garnish
Edible disco dust, as garnish

THE RECIPES

Muddle the apple well in mixing glass.
Add the rose petals and muddle gently.
Add ice and the remaining ingredients.
Shake well and double-strain into a
chilled coupe. Top with a single drop of
absinthe and a glittered rose petal.

gaz sez: *If you don't know Carol, then make it your business to meet her. She's delightful, crazy as a March Hare, and she* *has a smile that's unmatched in the industry. This drink is just about as complex as they come, and the layers of flavors contained within burst to life on the tongue, singing glorious arias all the way down the throat. Nice one, Carol.*

Pointy Reckoning

Adapted from a recipe by Claire Prideaux, Il Lido Italian Canteen, Cottesloe, Western Australia.

"At the Italian restaurant where I bartend, there is a mysterious and enormous stash of Liquore Strega. Nobody knows how long it has been there, or even who ordered such an unnecessary quantity. Consequently, for at least the last two years, we've been trying to dream up a cocktail using Strega so that we have a hope of using it all up sometime within the next two decades. Countless hours of Googling and consultation and experimentation took place, but we were never really all that happy with any of these creations, and the customers even less so.

"One day a couple of months ago, I was trawling Jeffrey Morgenthaler's recipes for probably the thirtieth time, but it was the first time I had really noticed that he combined Strega with cinnamon in the Autumn Leaves. From that pairing, the rest just seemed to come out of nowhere. Though if you know me, it's pretty predictable that I would choose rye whiskey as the base spirit, and I have an affection for Hellfire bitters that borders on obsessive. So really, I just combined a lot of my favourite things, and to hell with everyone else... but the result - simultaneously spicy, herbal and fresh - was surprisingly very well-received.

"The name is a wink to the Strega, which translates to "witch" in Italian. The bottles themselves are even labelled with a large sketch of a crone! I love drink names with a literary background, and the first thing that popped into my head when I thought about witchcraft was Arthur Miller's The Crucible. The name comes from a line uttered by the main antagonist, when she warns her friends that snitching on her to the authorities for practicing witchcraft will result in them being brought "a pointy reckoning in [their] sleep".

45 ml (1.5 oz) Wild Turkey 101 Rye
30 ml (1 oz) Liquore Strega
25ml (.85 oz) fresh lemon juice
25ml (.85 oz) cinnamon syrup*
1 dash Bitter Truth lemon bitters
1 dash Bittermens Hellfire bitters
Shake all ingredients well and strain into a chilled coupe glass.

*To make cinnamon syrup, add 1 cup white sugar to 1 cup just-boiled water and stir until dissolved; add 5 cinnamon quills and let steep for 3-4 hours. Remove quills and keep syrup in fridge until use.

gaz sez: *I love drinks with a good back-story, and this one sure as heck has that, but like Claire, I like to see Strega be put to good use, too, and she pulled this one off admirably. Nice one, Claire.*

Port of Spain

Adapted from a recipe by Kyle Mathis, Taste Bar, St. Louis, Missouri

30 ml (1 oz) Rittenhouse Rye
15 ml (1/2 oz.) Angostura aromatic bitters
15 ml (1/2 oz.) St. Elizabeth's All-spice Dram
22.5 ml (3/4 oz.) fresh lemon juice
22.5 ml (3/4 oz.) grenadine
22.5 ml (3/4 oz.) egg white

Combine all ingredients in shaker tin and dry shake to emulsify egg whites. Add ice and shake for 20 seconds. Fine strain into large coupe.

gaz sez: *Another poor bastard who Crazy Ted Kilgore has been influencing, huh? Paid off, though. And for my money it's the 1/2 oz of Angostura that makes this dram shine. And the rye, of course. And the All-Spice Dram. Whatever it is that pulls all these ingredients together doesn't really matter. What matters is that this is a very well-balanced quaff, and if Ted's drinking these, I'll join him at the bar any old day.*

Queen Anne's Revenge

Adapted from a recipe by Anthony DeSerio, Coastal Gourmet Group. Aspen Restaurant/Latitude 41 Shipyard Tavern, Mystic, CT.

"Working in a tavern in the oldest maritime museum in the country is rather inspiring. When I took over operations I made it a point to take a walk around. I could not help thinking I need rum drinks. Lots and lots of historic rum drinks. Where better to start than with the Daiquiri? I do have Grog and Bumboo, too, so I also paid a visit to Mr. Wayne Curtis and his book and a Bottle of Rum. Here is the result: My Daiquiri that pays homage to the notorious rum-drinking pirate Edward Teach, aka Blackbeard, who was said to add gunpowder to his rum and light it before consuming. I don't recommend this, but I honor this practice by using gunpowder green tea.

"I have also added a little modern variation as well, knowing one acceptable change to this cocktail was brought on when Hemingway added grapefruit and maraschino. I've altered this with blood orange and Domaine de Canton ginger. By adding the egg white foam (smoke) that adds to the texture, aroma, and appearance of this cocktail and gives a little credit to the man and his history." —Anthony DeSerio.

45 ml (1.5 oz) light rum
15 ml (.5 oz) Gunpowder Green Tea Simple Syrup*
15 ml (.5 oz) fresh lime juice
7.5 ml (.25 oz) blood orange juice

7.5 ml (.25 oz) Domaine de Canton
ginger liqueur
Ginger Tea Foam**, as garnish
1 lime slice, as garnish

Shake hard over ice and strain into a chilled rocks glass. Add the garnishes.

***Gunpowder Green Tea Simple Syrup**: Fill a pint glass halfway with demerara sugar. Set 3 gunpowder green teabags on top and fill the rest with hot water. Stir to dissolve the sugar (take the strings off the tea bags if they have them or they will intertwine with your barspoon!) and let steep for 3 to 5 minutes. Cool briefly, then refrigerate to thicken and cool completely.

**Ginger Tea Foam: Whisk 1 egg white in a medium bowl, slowly adding 7.5 ml (.25 oz) Gunpowder Green Tea Syrup and 7.5 ml (.25 oz) Domaine de Canton ginger liqueur. When firm, spoon on top of the cocktail as garnish.

gaz sez: *Okay, already, Anthony! We're impressed; we're impressed. And what a pain in the ass this was to put together—Ginger Tea Foam, indeed. The drink really rocks, though! It's almost like you know what you're doing . . .*

Ready Room

Adapted from a recipe by Christopher Day, Honeycut, Los Angeles

"*Nerd alert* Inspiration for this came from Captain Picard of Star Trek (TNG), who would always call private meetings in his "Ready Room," and who would also invariably order an Earl Grey tea from the replicator before he sat down to chat. I made this as an old fashioned variant of an Earl Grey tea." —Christopher Day

45 ml (1.5 oz) George Dickel No. 12
15 ml (.5 oz) Bowmore Legend Islay Scotch
15 ml (.5 oz) Amaro Montenegro
15 ml (.5 oz) Cocchi di Torino
2 dashes Miracle Mile Bergamot Bitters
1 lemon twist, as garnish
1 orange twist, as garnish

Stir over cracked ice, and strain into an old-fashioned glass with one large rock. Add the garnishes.

gaz sez: *Here we go again with a fabulous drink that sports not one, but two very different whiskeys—The first from Tennessee, the second, used as an accent, from Scotland. Add to these an amaro and a very distinctive Italian vermouth, and you have one very fine complex dram. Christopher, by the way, works with Honeycut co-owner Alex Day, but no, they aren't related.*

Red Barchetta

Adapted from a recipe by Mel James, BC's Kitchen, Lake St. Louis, MO.

"I created this cocktail for the 2012 Campari competition. It is quite special to me because it was the first cocktail that I created 100% on my own, with no help, opinions asked or input from anyone (and only my second competition at that point as well). It tied first place with Ted Kilgore, and the tie breaker ended up being our technical scores. I took second place and was beside myself thrilled - I had never expected to even place, and the fact that people enjoyed one of my cocktails brought me a joy that is beyond words." —Mel James.

2 strawberries, hulled
45 ml (1.5 oz) Campari
30 ml (1 oz) North Shore gin #6
30 ml (1 oz) The Big O ginger liqueur
7.5 ml (.25 oz) Cherry Heering
7.5 ml (.25 oz) premium aged balsamic vinegar
3 dashes Angostura orange bitters
1 strawberry speared with a small rosemary sprig, as garnish

Muddle the strawberries in a mixing glass, then add the remaining ingredients. Shake over ice and fine-strain into a chilled cocktail glass. Add the garnish.

gaz sez: *This is one of those recipes that shouldn't work, but it does. When I read it I nearly threw it into the circular file, but hey, it's got gin and Campari, right? I gave it a shot. It worked. I especially like the way the strawberries play with the balsamic in this one, and the ginger and cherry liqueurs dance well together, too, but it's the Campari/gin combination that holds this drink together, and the aromatic rosemary garnish adds a special something, too.*

Red Riding Hooch

Adapted from a recipe by Joseph Boley, Red House, Paris

"Our Autumn Negroni variation," —Joseph Boley

30 ml (1 oz) Beefeater gin
20 ml (.7 oz) apple-spice infused Dubonnet*
10 ml (.33 oz) Campari
10 ml (.33 oz) Averna
1 orange slice or twist, as garnish.

Build in a double old-fashioned glass, stir briefly, and add the garnish.

Methodology: build and garnish like a Negroni.

*Apple-Spice Infused Dubonnet

Add the peels from 3 apples, the zest of half a lemon, 2 cinnamon sticks, a teaspoon of allspice, and a teaspoon of coriander seeds (inspiration from the apple bitters recipe in Parsons' Bitters book). Smash allspice and coriander, put all ingredients into a jar with 1 liter of dubbonet. Let this sit for 5 days and filter.

gaz sez: *First off I should mention that the apple-spice infused Dubonnet is worthy of a glass all its own. Mix it with these other ingredients, though, and you have the makings of a masterpiece. I can't tell you just how much I loved this drink. Well done, Joe.*

Red Thorn Cocktail

Adapted from a recipe by Takumi Watanabe, The Sailing Bar, Kibi, Sakurai, Nara, Japan

45 ml (1.5 oz) Irish whiskey
30ml (1 oz) dry vermouth
15 ml (.5 oz) raspberry syrup
5 ml (.2 oz) fresh lemon juice
2 dashes Green Chartreuse
2 dashes absinthe
1 lemon twist, as garnish

Shake over ice and strain into a chilled cocktail glass. Add the garnish.

gaz sez: *Please please please take the time to make this drink. I first met Takumi Watanabe at Diageo's World Class bartender competition in Greece a few years back, and he made me the best Aviation I ever tasted. It's hard to get across to you just how good* the drink was, but the balance was so finely tuned that my first sip just knocked my socks off. His Red Thorn Cocktail is just as good. Takumi Watanabe is, beyond a shadow of a doubt, one of the very finest mixologists I ever met.

The Red Thorne was also detailed in Jared Brown and Anistatia Miller's book, The Deans Of Drink, *and Takumi tells me that Harry Johnson's Black Thorn cocktail was the inspiration for his Red Thorn. Johnson should feel honored.*

Roark's Laughter

Adapted from a recipe by Chris Harrington, Subject, NYC

"After countless years of making, shaking and sipping cocktails I had to come to admit that Root Beer is my favorite thing to drink in the whole world. I've finally figured out how to make cognac and genever taste as much like Stewarts Root Beer as possible. The drink was named after the first line in the book **The Fountainhead**. The character, Howard Roark, laughs and his laughter is supposed to represent a complete lack of worry or concern. It's the representation of calculated freedom and the absence of trouble in your mind. Root Beer. Root Beer reminds me of those sort of moments in childhood when you crack open an A&W and chase a bag of cheese fries during the summer months. School is over and your only concern in the world is how high you can climb a tree or something." —Chris Harrington.

1.25 oz Bols Genever
22.5 ml (.75 oz) Pierre Ferrand Cognac
15 ml (.5 oz) fresh lemon juice
22.5 ml (.75 oz) Root Beer Honey*
2 Dashes Aromatic Bitters**

Shake over ice and strain into an ice-filled old-fashioned glass.

***Root Beer Honey:** mix 16 oz clover honey and .125 oz root beer oil extract in 16 oz hot water. Mix well, allow to cool, and refrigerate.

**Aromatic Bitters: 50/50 Angostura/Fee Brothers Aromatic bitters

gaz sez: *And here we have the last recipe to be chosen* for this batch of 101 Best New Cocktails. Last, but certainly not least. We're going out with a bang this year. It's tough to describe this particular drink, but I think it might be the cognac that plays* referee to the genever and the root-beer in this one. Somehow these two ingredients throw punches till the end of round one, then decide to stop fighting, and circle the ring hand-in-hand, instead. Pretty impressive!

*This drink isn't the last alphabetically, but it was the 101st recipe to be chosen for this volume.

Rose Colored Glasses

Adapted from a recipe by Daniel Dufek, Hi Hat Lounge, Milwaukee, WI.

"Hey gaz, seeing as you've already tried this drink, I figured I'd throw it in the ring for the next edition of your book. Thanks!" —Daniel Dufek.

2 lemon twists (reserve 1 for garnish)
45 ml (1.5 oz) Plymouth gin
22.5 ml (.75 oz) Noilly Prat dry vermouth
7.5 ml (.25 oz) Lapsang Souchong Syrup*
2 dashes Angostura bitters
6 drops Bittercube Lemon Tree bitters

Stir over ice and strain into chilled coupe. Add the garnish.

*Lapsang Souchong Syrup: Brew tea at normal strength. Add an equal amount of granulated sugar. Stir until dissolved.

gaz sez: *I did, indeed, sample this drink. It was a finalist cocktail at a Plymouth Gin competition, and I tried it in Chicago when I was traveling with the good folk at Pernod-Ricard USA on the Pioneers of Mixology roadshow. The Lapsang Souchong Syrup is what really pulls this drink together, and the Plymouth provides a sturdy backbone that can easily support all the bitters here, without getting lost in the crowd.*

The Rusty Apple

Adapted from a recipe by Christopher James, The Ryland Inn, Whitehouse Station, NJ.

"This cocktail is intended to be a twisted, seasonal mash-up of an Apple Martini and a Rusty Nail," —Christopher James.

30 ml (1.0 oz) Chivas Regal scotch
45 ml (1.5 oz) Berentzen Apfelkorn
30 ml (1.0 oz) Honeycrisp apple juice
15 ml (.5 oz) fresh lemon juice
15 ml (.5 oz) agave nectar
Drambuie foam*
1 apple fan, as garnish
freshly grated cinnamon, as garnish

Dispense enough Drambuie foam to fill a chilled coupe glass 1/3 of the way. Shake the rest of the ingredients over ice and strain into the chilled coupe through one part of the foam to avoid ruining the separation effect. Finish off with an apple fan and some freshly grated cinnamon on the surface of the foam

*Drambuie Foam
60 ml (2 oz) Drambuie
30 ml (1 oz) Berentzen Apfelkorn
15 ml (.5 oz) lemon juice
4 egg whites

Add all ingredients to an ISI charger and use a single charge to whip it into a foam.

gaz sez: *I'm not a huge fan of Berentzen Apfelkorn, or at least I wasn't until I tasted this baby. The interaction between this apple-flavored liqueur and the Chivas Regal scotch is a joy to behold. Scotch can be so hard to work with, and Christopher James pulled this one off very handily, indeed. Nice one, Christopher.*

Sazeroni

Adapted from a recipe by René Förster, Twist Cocktail Bar, Innside, Dresden, Germany.

"This is my winning drink from the Liquid Art Competition in Germany. It is a combination from Sazerac and Negroni. Peter Dorelli, one of the judges, said, 'This is a marriage made in heaven,'" —René Förster.

Tabu Absinth Classic Strong, as a rinse
40 ml (1.33 oz) Remy Martin VSOP
20 ml (.7 oz) Cinzano Orancio

20 ml (.7 oz) Campari
1 dash The Bitter Truth Grapefruit Bitters
1 orange twist, as a garnish
1 grapefruit twist, as a garnish

Rinse a chilled old-fashioned glass with the absinthe and add a large ice-ball or ice-cube. Stir the rest of the ingredients over ice and strain into the glass. Add the garnishes.

gaz sez: *I'm certainly not going to argue with Peter Dorelli about this drink. It's a sterling mixture of two fine cocktails. I admit to not using Tabu Absinth Classic Strong as a rinse, since I just couldn't find it in the USA (I used Pernod Absinthe instead), but now that I know about Tabu, I'm dying to try it next time I'm in Germany. And Cinzano Orancio was new to me, too, but I managed to get my hands on a bottle of this stuff (thanks, Pete), and it's a pretty incredible orange-flavored vermouth that will, no doubt, become a frequently used ingredient in the not-too-distant future. Apologies to René for these digressions--the Sazeroni is f*ckin' awesome, René, and that's a killer smile you have on your face, too! Keep up the good work.*

Sencha Flip

Adapted from a recipe by Jason Walsh, CocktailLogic.com, Brooklyn, NY.

"This cocktail was inspired by my adoration of Sencha Japanese tea. Many people use Matcha, however Sencha has more complexity and flavor so I prefer it over Matcha in certain cocktails." —Jason Walsh.

60 ml (2 oz) Plymouth gin
45 ml (1.5 oz) Sweetened Sencha green tea (chilled)
22.5 ml (.75 oz) fresh lemon juice
1 large egg white

Dry-shake, then add a few ice cubes (not too many) and shake again. Strain into a chilled glass (I use a desert wine glass or pony) and enjoy.

gaz sez: *Sencha or Matcha? Matcha or Sencha? It's one of those choices that needs a damned good ponder. Jason called it well here!*

Siam Saoco

Adapted from a recipe by Iain McPherson, Panda and Sons, Edinburgh, Scotland

"The inspiration for my cocktail the Siam Saoco (Sa-oh-ko) comes from my childhood family memories. You can never relive your memories but you can always cherish them

"I wanted to create a cocktail that would be unique and bring a flavour profile that would get my guests thinking about the taste and enjoying it and a cocktail that would really showcase the Bacardi. A drink to me is not just about the flavour, the experience is very important too. I wanted to get my customers relating to my stories to their own so not only will they enjoy my cocktail they will also enjoy remembering personal memories from long ago and even better the ones they had forgotten about. Slainte!" —Iain McPherson

50ml (1.7 oz) Bacardi Superior
50ml (1.7 oz) Foco roasted coconut water
4 Thai sweet basil leaves
Barspoon light agave nectar
Pinch Himalayan salt

Shake over ice and fine strain into a chilled cocktail glass or coupette.

gaz sez: *Another bow to the Gods of simplicity here, and Iain pulls it off admirably. Note, also, the pinch of salt in this drink. It makes a heck of a difference, adding another dimension and highlighting the basil notes. Well done, Iain.*

Smokey Ol' Scribe

Adapted from a recipe by Tim Robinson, Twist, London.

"This cocktail—one of the 2 winners of Luxardo Masters of Maraschino 2012—began life as a variation on The Last Word, using standard Maraschino and Green Chartreuse. I then picked up a lovely bottle of vintage Maraschino and started playing around - I found that it had a richer, earthier marzipan profile than the standard non-vintage bottling which the Green Chartreuse overwhelmed. The V.E.P. bottling of the Yellow is more subtle than the Green but has plenty of depth which stands up to the amazing powerful smokey notes of the Tobala. The D&B bitters bring out the sweeter and herbal notes while my Black Pepper syrup finishes it off with a healthy kick which accentuates the cherry of the Vintage Maraschino which is very much the star of the piece." —Tim Robinson.

20ml (.66 oz) Vintage Maraschino Liqueur (approx 1975)
25ml (.85 oz) V.E.P. Yellow Chartreuse
25ml (.85 oz) Del Maguey Tobala (Wild Mountain) Mezcal
25ml (.85 oz) fresh lime juice
10ml black pepper syrup*
15ml egg white
Spritz Dandelion & Burdock Bitters
long tightly-curled twists of lemon & lime, as garnish

Spritz the inside of a chilled coupe with

the bitters using an atomizer. Dry shake all the ingredients except bitters, then shake again with cubed ice. Double strain into the prepared chilled coupe, and add the garnishes.

* Black Pepper Syrup
200ml (6.75 oz) water
200gm (7 Oz) white sugar
40gm (1.4 oz) black peppercorns
5g (.15 oz) cardamom pods (cracked)
5g (.15 oz) coriander seeds
10ml (.33 oz) vodka
15ml (.5 oz) fresh lemon juice

Bring the water to the boil, then crack the peppercorns, cardamom & coriander and add to the water. Simmer for 30minutes then remove from heat. Once the pot is cool to touch strain the peppercorns and discard. Return the spice-infused water to the pan and bring it up to a gentle simmer. Add the sugar and remove from heat and stir until dissolved. When the syrup has cooled, add the vodka and lemon juice and bottle the syrup in an airtight container.

gaz sez: *Well done, Tim. You managed to confuse me to all hell. I'm quite sure that your version of this drink is far better than the one that I was able to make using regular maraschino and regular Yellow Chartreuse, but my version was pretty damned fabulous all on its own. Your black-pepper syrup is bloody divine, too. Thought I should mention that.*

Smokin' Hopps

Adapted from a recipe by Seth Laufman, Burritt Room, San Francisco, CA.

"Refreshing and unique." —Seth Laufman.

60 ml (2 oz) Vida Mezcal
15 ml (.5 oz) simple syrup (rich)
15 ml (.5 oz) fresh lemon juice
15 ml (.5 oz) Licor 43
60 ml (2 oz) India Pale Ale

Shake and strain the first four ingredients into chilled fizz glass. Top with the ale.

gaz sez: *Oh. My. God. How damned weird can you get? I don't think I could spend much time in Seth's head, but I have to hand it to him-he came off with one very original drink here. And it works, too. Well done, young man.*

South of Heaven

Adapted from a recipe by George Megalokonomos, Food Mafia, Glyfada, Athens, Greece.

"This is my winning cocktail for the Skinos Mediterranean Cocktail Challenge, 2013. I wanted to create a unique and simple cocktail with this great spirit (Skinos Mastiha) without using juices, syrups or infusions. The bitter sweet taste is very balanced and the complexity is remarkable! also the aromas from the combination of spirits, mint and lime is excellent!" — George Megalokonomos,

50ml (1.7 oz) Skinos Mastiha Spirit
30 ml (1 oz) Cocchi Americano
15 ml (.5 oz) Fernet Branca
3-4 dashes The Bitter Truth's celery bitters

Stir all the ingredients for 10 seconds in an ice-filled mixing glass and strain into a chilled martini glass. Garnish with a lime zest and a mint sprig (smack it with your hands before placing in the surface of the drink).

*"To create Skinos Mastiha Liqueur, the Mastiha tree is harvested for its resin once per year in the months of June and July. Small cuts are made in the tree bark which releases small amounts of resin that are collected over ten to twenty days. It is then transferred to the village in wooden casks where the highest quality Mastiha is selected and cleaned. After distillation sugar, alcohol and mineral water are added, resulting in a distinctive, balanced spirit with pronounced notes of cucumber, pine, anise and fresh herbs." San Francisco World Spirits Competition 2011.

gaz sez: *This Mastiha liqueur sure is funky—and I mean that in a good way—so when you marry it to Cocchi, Fernet, and celery bitters, it's hard to predict what the result will be. My take on the drink is that, it's right up my alley, and although this one won't appeal to everyone, if you enjoy funky, this drink's for you. Make mine a double, please.*

Spanish Inquisition

Adapted from a recipe by Scott Diaz, Elliott's Oyster House, Seattle, WA.

"I am the Beverage Manager for Elliott's Oyster House in Seattle, but I still get behind the wood quite often at the restaurant. I wanted to create a full-bodied, and rich craft cocktail that showcased the wonderful flavors of raisin, bitter orange, and almond notes. Be sure to properly measure the ingredients for this one, especially the sherry, as too much can make for a sickeningly sweet concoction. Cheers!" —Scott Diaz.

22.5 ml (.75 oz) Lustau Pedro Ximenez sherry
22.5 ml (.75 oz) Aperol
15 ml (.5 oz) Averna amaro
30 ml (1 oz) fresh blood orange juice
1 teaspoon orgeat syrup
1 orange twist, as garnish

Shake over ice and strain into a chilled coupe. Flame the twist over the drink, then add as garnish.

gaz sez: *I never expected a Spanish Inquisition . . . This one's like Forest Gump's box of chocolates—you never know what's coming next! The Aperol hits first, then it's the sherry, the n the Averno take charge, and the orgeat has her say, too. A complex dram is this one. Nicely done, Scott.*

St. Joseph's

Adapted from a recipe by Chris Hannah, French 75 Bar, New Orleans

"St. Joseph's Day is an interesting holiday in New Orleans. We have a lot of Catholic Churches building Food Altars for the holiday and it's to recognize St. Joseph for providing food to the Sicilian immigrants while they were suffering when arriving in New Orleans in the early 1800's. So, I created this digestive cocktail and I figured that St. Joseph's is a good name for it. If you've ever seen pictures of a New Orleanian Food Altar you'd understand." —Chris Hannah

30 ml (1 oz) Cynar
15 ml (.5 oz) Aperol
15 ml (.5 oz) Averna
15 ml (.5 oz) Pedro Ximenez sherry
1 orange twist, as garnish

Stir over ice and strain into an ice-filled brandy snifter. Add the garnish.

gaz sez: *Chris also submitted a recipe that he created for Alex Day, one of my partners in the gaz bar project, but this St Joseph's cocktail really tickled my fancy. It's a great demonstration of what can be done if you really know your ingredients. Few people would put all four of these items together in one glass, but they party together really well, the sherry acting as a dance partner for all three of the bitters in this drink. You're a class act, Chris Hannah.*

Strega Sour

Adapted from a recipe by Junior Ryan, Clyde Common, Portland, OR.

"I won the international Martin Miller Trade It Up Competition last year with this recipe." —Junior Ryan.

45 ml (1.5 oz) Martin Miller's Westbourne Strength gin
22.5 ml (.75 oz) Strega
22.5 ml (.75 oz) fresh lemon juice
15 ml (.5 oz) egg whites
1 teaspoon Earl Grey honey syrup (2:1)
4 to 5 drops Angostura bitters, as garnish

Dry-shake, then add ice and shake again. Strain into a chilled cocktail glass. Drizzle or use a dropper to add the bitters in an attractive pattern on the foam.

gaz sez: *I put this one into my column in the* San Francisco Chronicle. *Here's part of what I wrote about it:*

Strega liqueur is one of those herbal potions, flavored with just under 70 herbs and spices, and created in the mid-1800s. Nineteenth-century producers were fond of making herbal potions, Bénédictine being another great example of this sort of liqueur.

Some of the botanicals used to flavor Strega are said to be juniper, mint, saffron, fennel, and cinnamon. It's a complex dram that can tear a drink down to its foundations unless it's used judiciously. I've always had a fondness for Strega, though I've usually sipped it as a post-prandial potion as opposed to a cocktail ingredient.

Junior Ryan . . . is a judicious sort of cocktailian. He knows how to use Strega well. Calms it down with a healthy tot of strong gin, he does, and it works a treat. Why didn't I think of that? When in doubt, add gin. It's a good rule of thumb.

A Tale of Two Roberts

Adapted from a recipe by Frank Caiafa, Peacock Alley, The Waldorf=Astoria, New York City.

"At Peacock Alley, we have debuted our Robert Burns Cocktail. It's a hybrid of the Old Waldorf Bar Book recipe which is essentially a Rob Roy with Absinthe, and the Bobby Burns, from the *Old Savoy Cocktail Book*, which is equal parts scotch, sweet vermouth, and a bit of Bénédictine.

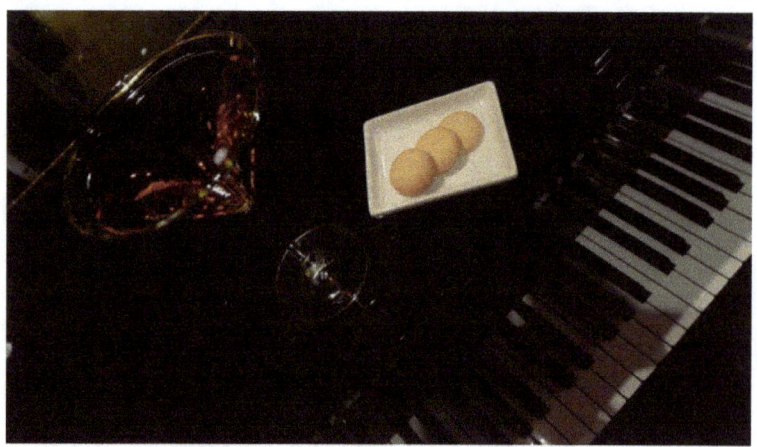

"I did not add (orange) bitters to this version as I feel the drink is complex enough and the bitters helped to muddy up the mix. To happily confuse things more, I asked the Waldorf=Astoria pastry kitchen to make shortbread cookies as a garnish (thanks, guys!).

"I think the small changes makes big differences (and the finish is awesome!). Enjoy!" —Frank Caiafa.

67.5 ml (2.25 oz) Sheep Dip 8-Year-Old blended scotch whisky
37.5 ml (1.25 oz) sweet vermouth
10 ml (.33 oz) Bénédictine
6 dashes Pernod/Absinthe Mix*
1 lemon twist, as garnish
2 shortbread cookies, as garnish

Stir over ice and strain into a chilled cocktail glass. Add the garnishes: twist to the cocktail, cookies on a plate on the side.

*Pernod/Absinthe Mix: Ratio is 2/3 Pernod and 1/3 La Muse Verte Absinthe.

gaz sez: *Here's a sort of modified Bobby Burns that works so very well, indeed. Made with a great scotch, the addition of absinthe makes this one stand head and shoulders above the original.*

10 Bloods

Adapted from a recipe by Kelvin Wood, The Soul, Guangzhou, Guangdong Province, China.

"This is the cocktail I created for the World Class Kick Off in South China, 2013. The name is comes from T-10 (Tanqueray No.TEN) and using Peychaud's bitters as the color. The story behind the cocktail is also about "10 years" experience for me ... The Plum liqueur & the Monin Rose syrup release the sweetness to balance the Campari & the bitters ... [It]smells & taste like a perfume, a little bit spicy from the tongue, the finish is extremely long & strong as layer by layer the flavor comes out," —Kelvin Wood.

45 ml (1.5 oz) Tanqueray No.TEN
15 ml (.5 oz) Luxardo Plum Liqueur
5 ml (1 teaspoon) Campari
5 ml (1 teaspoon) Monin Rose Syrup
10 ml (2 teaspoons) Peychaud's Bitters
1 pink grapefruit twist, as garnish

Stir over ice and strain into a chilled sherry glass. Add the garnish.

gaz sez: *(I couldn't get hold of the Luxardo plum liqueur so I used the Prucia brand instead.) This is quite simply one of the best gin cocktails I've ever tasted. It's like the climax of the 1812 Overture in a glass. Splendid.*

Third Day in Taipei

Adapted from a recipe created by Aaron Feder when he designed the cocktail menu at OUNCE Taipei, Taiwan.

"A super smokey and lightly peaty scotch cocktail with just a kiss of bitter orange. The glass is filled with smoke from barrel ageing sticks just before it is served. It is the house cocktail at "OUNCE" Taipei in Taiwan. I designed their cocktail program and trained all the bartenders from scratch in Western style classic cocktails during the life of my contract. I wrote the cocktail on my third day in the country and it quickly became the favorite." —Aaron Feder

45 ml (1.5 oz) Oban 14-yr-old scotch
15 ml (.5 oz) Talisker scotch
45 ml (1.5 oz) Ferrand Dry Curacao
2 dashes Angostura bitters
2 dashes Regan's orange bitters No. 6
1 Barrel aged cocktail stick (http://tuthilltown.gostorego.com/barrel-aged-cocktail-kit-refill.html)

Stir spirits and bitters over ice. Use a torch to light the age stick; blow out the flame and hold a snifter upside down over the stick to fill it with smoke. Now quickly strain the cocktail into the smoke filled glass in front of the guest.

gaz sez: *I knew nothing of these aging sticks until I saw this recipe. They're pretty nifty, I think, though I haven't had time to experiment with them as aging agents. I love Aaron's ingenuity that drove him to set fire to these things, though! The make-up of the rest of this drink is, I believe, a sign of things to come. Mixing and matching different bottlings of scotch seems to be quite the way to go these days. Aaron pulled this off admirably.*

The Trainspotter

Adapted from a recipe by Thomas Newcomb, The Continental Room, Fullerton, CA

"This original cocktail is my twist on the classic Brooklyn cocktail. The name has no direct relevance to the cocktail but hey, Trainspotting was/is an amazing film so there." — Thomas Newcomb.

60 ml (2 oz) Dickel Rye
22.5 ml (.75 oz) St. Germain
15 ml (.5 oz) Cherry Heering
7.5 ml (.25 oz) Fernet Branca
1 Grapefruit twist, as garnish

Stir over ice and strain into a chilled cocktail glass. Add the garnish.

gaz sez: *Once again, it's the Fernet that brings everything together in this drink, and the Dickel Rye provides a sturdy backbone—nicely done, Thomas.*

Trinity Avenue

Adapted from a recipe by Mark Holmes, Vanilla Rooms, Cardiff, Welsh Wales

"The crème de banane helps to smooth out this bitters-heavy drink wonderfully, adding a exotic Caribbean twist to a somewhat classic style drink. The drink is named for the road on which the house of Angostura can be found today."
—Mark Holmes.

45 ml (1.5 oz) Angostura 1919 rum
15 ml (.5 oz) Dubonnet Rouge
15 ml (.5 oz) crème de banane
7.5 ml (.25 oz or 12 dashes) Angostura Aromatic Bitters
1 orange twist, as an aromatic garnish
1 dehydrated banana chip, as garnish

Stir over ice and strain into a chilled cocktail glass. Express orange oil over the top of the drink and discard the twist. Add the dehydrated banana chip.

gaz sez: *Yet another bitters-laden cocktail. Makes my little heart glad, it does. And Mark is right on the money when he points to the crème de bananes as the ingredient that balances out the bitters. Fabulous job, Mark, and I must add that I love the relative simplicity of this formula—it's one of those drinks that can be made in near-as-damn-it every bar in the world. I hope that the good folk at Angostura take note.*

Trott On

Adapted from a recipe by **Nick Koumbarakis, Orphanage, Cape Town, Western Province, South Africa.**

"I serve the drink accompanied with a side serving of high quality dark chocolate and orange served in a small bamboo bowl." —Nick Koumbarakis.

4 green cardamom pods (reserve 1 for garnish)
45 ml (1.5 oz) Johnnie Walker Green Label scotch whisky
20 ml (.66 oz) Bols white crème de cacao
20 ml (.66 oz) fresh lemon juice
20 ml (.66 oz) Rooibos Infused Syrup*

5 ml (.17 oz) Grand Marnier
1 orange twist, as garnish

Muddle the cardamom in a mixing glass. Add ice and the remaining ingredients. Shake and fine-strain into a vintage stainless steel coupe. Add the garnishes.

*Rooibos Infused Syrup: Using a 1:1 ratio, add 500 ml (about 2 cups) water to a sizeable pan and bring to a boil. Add 500 g (2.5 cups) castor (superfine) sugar, then reduce the heat to the lowest possible setting. Stir until the sugar dissolves. Add 8 to 9 organic Rooibos teabags, for maximum infusion allow teabags to settle for 20 to 30 minutes, stirring every 10 minutes. Cool to room temperature, then strain into a clean bottle and refrigerate. To prevent the formation of sugar crystallization an emulsifying ingredient known as gum arabic can be added.

gaz sez: *I loves me some cardamom, that's for sure—check out my orange bitters if you don't believe me. And this drink comes together so damned well in the glass, the Johnnie Walker Green Label scotch serving as a fabulous base. And if you've never tasted Rooibos tea, here's your chance to experience something really special. Nicely done, Nick. This drink is well worth the shout-out.*

23-year-old Girl

Adapted from a recipe by **Foxyie Wong**, The Soul, Guangzhou, Guangdong Province, China.

"This is my cocktail awarded the champion in 2012 Bacardi Legacy Cocktail Competition China Final in January, 2013.

It is said in Cuba that Rum can turn a girl from as cold as marble to be tender and soft as water, especially the Bacardi Superior Light Rum, with the pure sugarcane flavor as well as its smooth characteristic. This cocktail is a birthday present for my 23-year-old ex-girlfriend. Having just graduated from college, she has been working hard for herself and her family. She felt tired and lost. Through this cocktail I hope her to keep the pureness, spotlessness and dreams inside her heart no matter what troubles may happen in the reality.

So when you taste this cocktail, you may feel very special flavour in the beginning while the fresh after tasting. What's more, when some drinkers taste this cocktail, they may be moved by the story and even recall their memories when they were fallen in love in the past time." Foxyie Wong.

Ground black pepper, to rim half of a chilled cocktail glass
20 grams (just under 1 ounce) fresh cucumber cubes
45 ml (1.5 oz) Bacardi Superior Light Rum
10 ml (.33oz) fresh lemon juice
30 ml (1 0z) tomato juice
30 ml (1 oz) Touareg (Mint) Tea Syrup*
1 cucumber peel twist, as garnish
Gently muddle the cucumber cubes in a shaker. Add ice and the rest of the ingredients. Shake well and double strain into the pre-prepared glass. Add the garnish.

* Touareg (Mint) Tea Syrup
Dissolve 2 cups of sugar into one cup of hot, brewed Touareg tea. Allow to cool and refrigerate.

gaz sez: *How many people create drinks for their ex-girlfriends, huh? Nice touch, Foxyie! Nice drink, too, with a very unusual combination of ingredients. Tomato juice and mint tea together in the same glass? Who'd have thunk it? Works very well indeed, though. Foxyie, I think, is a bartender we'll hear much more about in the future.*

A Two-Fold Operation

Adapted from a recipe by Phoebe Esmon, Emmanuelle, Philadelphia.

"A good sherris-sack hath a two-fold operation in it"
—Falstaff, *Henry IV*, by William Shakespeare

60 ml (2 oz) Genever
22.5 ml (.75 oz) calvados
15 ml (.5 oz) oloroso sherry
15 ml (.5 oz) Bénédictine
1 dash Dale DeGroff's Pimento Aromatic Bitters

Stir over ice and strain into a chilled coupe.

gaz sez: *How unusual for Ms. Esmon to come up with a curious drink such as this one . . . I've no idea how she keeps doing this, but Phoebe keeps hitting that nail on the head over and over again. Nice one, Phoebe.*

Vakantie

Adapted from a recipe by Cynthia Turner, The Magnetic Field, Asheville, North Carolina.

"This cocktail simply reminded me of an exotic vacation. I chose the Dutch word [for *vacation*] and then.....made another." —Cynthia Turner.

Green Chartreuse, as a rinse.
45 ml (1.5 oz) Bols Genever
15 ml (.5 oz) Angostura 1919 rum
22.25 ml (.75 oz) fresh lemon juice

22.25 ml (.75 oz) orgeat

Shake over ice and strain into a chilled Green Chartreuse-rinsed coupe. No garnish.

gaz sez: *Well Jiminy Cricket this is a fine cocktail, indeed. Smoky, nutty, herby, you name it. It's all over the place. And it's also very finely tuned. Well done, Cynthia.*

War of the Roses

Adapted from a recipe by Nick Caputo, The Priory Tavern, London

"A modern take on the Clover Club using the contemporary Beefeater 24. Using a green oolong tea as the base for the fresh raspberry syrup and a different citrus, it highlights the qualities of the gin's unique character and gives a modern fresh take on an old classic. Although I didn't enter it into this year's Beefeater Competition it was my idea to take a classic Clover Club (i am still searching for someone that dislikes the drink :)) and twisting it to fit the gin—playing on the history of the gin, the cocktail and America's role on cocktail history.

"My idea started with the basic drink, replacing the citrus and with grapefruit to bring out that clean fresh note in 24, then using oolong to work with the raspberries which gives it that crisp fresh grassy spice and earthy profile which pushes the juniper and gin to the forefront whilst still being balanced and refreshing. The Lillet rosé was added to give it some complexity and depth on the finish; to tie the citrus, earthy juniper and tannin from tea, making the flavour linger.

"In terms of the name I liked the idea of the cocktail boom in America pre prohibition when the Clover Club first said to have been created and the great rivalry America and Britain always had pre 1900's. The idea that Gin was typically a British thing and the American's were using it to create such beautiful libations - it felt natural especially since James's Burrough's Beefeater was one of the most iconing London Dry Gin's available to twist it with 24. Using its botanicals to highlight its strengths and show the modernization in gin by altering this classic to fit.

"The tea in particular being something that the British were known for after first getting tea from the orient originally as green tea but by the time it returned home it was dried and black. So when Beefeater's Master Distiller incorporated this into Beefeater 24 by using Japanese Sensha tea and Chinese Green tea in its production, it was something to highlight the great journey of tea export Britain had by using it in the drink, almost reflecting the gin's travel to America through its own export.

"So this rivalry and history brought me to the name War of the Roses... it uses traditional ingredients in a modern way, illustrates two great nations rivalry and coming together to create tasty drinks and also nods to Britain's heritage." — Nick Caputo

50 ml (1.7 oz) Beefeater 24 gin
25 ml (.85 oz) fresh white grapefruit juice
25 ml (.85 oz) oolong green tea raspberry syrup*
10ml (.33 oz) Lillet rosé
1 egg white
1 lemon twist, as an aromatic garnish
1 lemon twist, as an aromatic garnish
rose petals, as garnish

Dry shake, add ice and shake hard. Strain into a chilled coupette and add the aromatic garnishes, discarding the twists after expressing their oils onto the drink. Sprinkle rose petals around the drink for garnish.

*Oolong Green Tea Raspberry Syrup

Brew 1 cup of oolong green tea in a small saucepan. Add 1 cup of fresh raspberries, and cook on low heat till the raspberries dissipate. Add 1 cup of caster (superfine) sugar, stir until the sugar dissolves, and strain the syrup through a double layer of dampened cheesecloth. Store in the refrigerator.

gaz sez: *Yeah, right, what Nick said. This is the second green-tea drink I've loved this year. Pretty astounding when you consider that I hate green tea...*

Ward 9

Adapted from a recipe by Jinjur Van Vogelpoel, Red House, Paris.

"This drink was created for a New Orleans themed cocktail night we did, and follows along the Last Word/Final Ward lines, named the Ward 9 after the New Orleans neighborhood that was gutted by Katrina," —Jinjur Van Vogelpoel

25 ml (.85 oz) Rye Whiskey
20 ml (.7 oz) Green Chartreuse
15 ml (.5 oz) St. Germain
20 ml (.7 oz) fresh lemon juice
egg white (approx 20 ml/.7 oz)
3 dashes Parfait Amour or good crème de violette*

Dry shake, then shake with ice and strain into a chilled "small high ball". (In France we have these elegant, tall pastis glasses which hold about 200 ml/7 oz*) Top with 3 dashes of Parfait Amour or good crème de violette.

* "The Parfait Amour is a bit tricky. Originally we were using a bizarre old brand of which the name escapes me and that seems to have vanished off the face of the earth (we found it in a dusty old liquor store in Paris along with Creme de Noyaux and all sorts of rare goodies). This particular Parfait Amour was extremely floral and violet-esque, and which no

other brand we've tried has matched. I suggest therefore, that it be replaced with a good Crème de Violette instead, as the drops on top are more to add fragrance and an extra touch of weirdness than anything else," —Jinjur Van Vogelpoel

gaz sez: *I have to be honest here: Anyone with a name like Jinjur Van Vogelpoel will be included in 101 BNC. It's too good of a name to pass on. And he works at Red House, one of my* *fave joints in Paris. Add to this the fact that the Ward 9 is a damned spectacular drink—the Parfait Amour/Crème de Violette aromatic garnish will just blow you away—and you have a dead certainty.*

The Westie

Adapted from a recipe by Fredo Ceraso, Loungerati, New York City.

"I developed this cocktail as an ode to the classic ingredients in the 'old man' drink— Drambuie and Galliano. Cocktails like the Harvey Wallbanger and the Rusty Nail evolved at a time when notorious tough guys like The Westies gang occupied Hell's Kitchen bar stools. They drank hard but with flair. The Westie captures this feeling. After all, though a cocktail should be well-balanced and thought out, it never hurts to have a good story behind it. (Read the full story of the drink here.) I have also submitted this drink for the 2012 Loungerati section of the award-winning cocktail menu at the Blythswood Square Hotel, Glasgow." —Fredo Ceraso.

22.5 ml (.75 oz) Redbreast 12 Year Old Pot Still Irish whiskey
22.5 ml (.75 oz) Drambuie
22.5 ml (.75 oz) Liquore Galliano L'Autentico
22.5 ml (.75 oz) fresh lemon juice
3 drops Dutch's Colonial Cocktail bitters (or Angostura in a pinch)
1 Bada Bing cherry, as garnish

Shake over ice for 15 to 20 seconds and double-strain into a chilled cocktail glass. Add the garnish.

gaz sez: *I'm a big fan of Redbreast so I had to try this one, and I was out of Dutch's Colonial Cocktail bitters so I used Angostura, just like Fredo suggested. Result? Fabulous. The addition of Liquore Galliano L'Autentico was a stroke of genius.*

Where There's Smoke There's Fire

Adapted from a recipe by Leslie Ross, Virtuoso Selections, Austin, TX

"This drink represents where I'm from, Houston Texas. It shows the cohesion of culture that coalesces in the form of Tex Mex Paradilla (Mixed Grill) and Texas mesquite BBQ, and THE drink of Mexico, the Paloma. The Anejo tequila has the body to stand up to the smoke and grilled flavors, the barrel aged agave really shines with the mesquite . The smoke also compliments the citrus, with every single ingredient bringing something to the completed cocktail. I won the Houston USBG Don Julio Comp with this drink, and am now headed to NYC to fight for the National Title. Fingers are crossed! I hope you guys enjoy it!" —Leslie Ross

45 ml (1.5 oz) mesquite-smoked Don Julio Anejo Tequila
22.5 ml (.75 oz) Combier Pamplemousse Liqueur
15 ml (.5 oz) Grilled Lime Juice
15 ml (.5 oz) Grilled Pink Grapefruit Juice
Jarritos Toronja Grapefruit Soda
Cilantro Mousse

Garnish with a wedge of Grilled and Smoked Grapefruit, drizzled with house made BBQ Habanero Shrub

Smoking the Tequila: Fill a large metal bowl with crushed or pelleted ice and nest a slightly smaller metal bowl, filled with tequila, inside it. Place your bowl at the very top of the smoker and sample every 5 minutes or so, it shouldn't take more than 15 minutes to get the right amount, anymore and that will be all that you can taste.

Grilled Fruit Juice: Ready to nerd out? Awesome! This particular step involves caramelization and the Maillard Reaction (go ahead and google that). After cutting up the limes and grapefruits into wedges, (more surface are = better flavor results) gently toss them in vanilla sugar and salt. Whole split vanilla beans in a half and half mix of white and turbinado sugar is what I use, and a pinch of highly salenic salt, like Maldon Sea Salt. Allow fruit to macerate, and once the juices and oils start to come out, grill them on a charcoal grill. Juice them while they are warm.

Cilantro Mousse Puree fresh cilantro with just enough water to make a liquid, strain the solids out with cheesecloth, and place into an ISI whipped cream charger with powdered Soy Lecithin. Use one Nitrogen Charger and shake. OK, now that science class is over, let's make this Paloma happen!

Shake the first 4 ingredients over ice and strain into an ice-filled Highball or Collins glass. (It needs to be narrow and tall, this way the Mousse stands). Top with the Jarritos Toronja Soda, leaving about 2 fingers of room at the top for the Mousse. Add the mousse and place a cilantro leaf on top, as garnish.

I choose to garnish this drink on the side, with a wedge of grilled and smoked grapefruit, and drizzle it with BBQ Habanero Shrub. Take the first sip without a straw to feel the drink come through all of the layers, enjoy the mingling textures, THEN use a straw if you want. After about half way, eat the piece of grapefruit.

gaz sez: *This is a fabulous example of just how far some 21st-century bartenders have pushed the craft, and it comes in the form of a splendid drink in which every facet is detectable, and everything comes together in harmony. Well done, Leslie.*

Wildbret

Adapted from a recipe by Reinhard Pohorec, The American Bar at The Savoy Hotel, London.

"First I'll point out that **Wildbret** is the German word for "game" or "venison," so the name's connected to Jägermeister—***Master of the Hunt***—one of the ingredients in the drink. What fascinates me about Wildbret this drink is the harmony of the ingredients, which might seem to be shuffled together quite randomly at the first sight. But with Wildbret, the whole drink is definitely more than just the sum of its parts.

This drink shows different aspects and facets with every sip and I chose to serve it up, so that the increasing temperature also contributes to a fascinating journey in the glass. You can play around slightly with floral or fruity bitters (Teapot Bitters in particular or Orange Bitters fit in very well) and your choice of whisky will also provide you with room for experimentation," —Reinhard Pohorec.

45ml (1.5 oz) Jägermeister
25ml (.85 oz) smoky, peaty, cask-strength Islay scotch whisky (i personally recommend Ardbeg Corryvreckan)
30ml (1 oz) Calvados
1 dash Boker's Bitters
2 dashes Dr. Adam Elmegirab's Aphrodite Bitters
1 lemon twist, as garnish

Stir over hand carved ice, and strain into a chilled coupette or cocktail glass. Add the garnish.

gaz sez: *Rieni (his nickname), certainly knows how to push my buttons. He and I worked together at the Jägermeister booth at the Berlin Bar Conference in 2012, so he knows that I love my Jäger, and then he goes and pairs it with a smoky, peaty, cask-strength scotch . . . Sneaky bastard! This drink comes together beautifully. Keep your eye on Reinhard Pohorec. He's an Austrian force to be reckoned with.*

Windsor Knot

Adapted from a recipe by Richard Yarnall, Orange County Bartenders' Cabinet, CA.

"This drink was conceptualized on the fly for a guest at the bar one night. He wanted something with bourbon that's bitter. I thought I'd try this Vieux Carre riff as the cognac sweetens up the rye and makes it feel more "bourbon-y." The recipe was refined in the coming weeks with the help of a few friends. The guest's name was Doug. The friends are Proprietors. Thanks guys."

Photo: Joey Maloney

30 ml (1 oz) Pierre Ferrand 1840 cognac
30 ml (1 oz) George Dickel Rye
15 ml (.5 oz) Dolin Dry Vermouth
15 ml (.5 oz) Cynar
1 tsp Bénédictine

Stir all ingredients over ice and strain into a chilled cocktail glass. Garnish with an orange peel.

gaz sez: *Right up my alley is this drink. Not an ingredient out of place—this sucker is perfectly executed, brilliantly balanced, and a damned good quaff to boot. Nicely done, Richard.*

Yes Man

Adapted from a recipe by **Scott Kennedy, Rubirosa,** New York City.

"A variation on a perfect Rob Roy, this blends classic spirits into a masculine sipper that's quick to please." —Scott Kennedy.

1 generous lemon twist
45 ml (1.5 oz) Johnnie Walker Black Label scotch whisky
15 ml (.5 oz) Dolin Blanc vermouth

15 ml (.5 oz) Dolin Rouge vermouth
shy 15 ml (.5 oz) Luxardo maraschino liqueur
1 dash Peychaud's bitters
1 skewered brandied cherry, as garnish

Rub the inside of a chilled coupe with the lemon twist, then discard. Stir over ice and strain into the glass. Add the garnish.

gaz sez: *This one's right up my alley. Big, strong, complex, and that one dash of Peychaud's brings the whole darned thing to life. Great job, Scott!*

www.ingramcontent.com/pod-product-compliance
Lightning Source LLC
Chambersburg PA
CBHW071112160426
43196CB00013B/2552